MW00634332

Loving Well Through Life's Storms

Weatherly LOVE

Estelle H. Herndon

Paperback ISBN-13: 978-1-948026-76-5
Digital ISBN-13: 978-1-948026-77-2
Notebook: 978-1-948026-78-9

Published by TMP Books, 3 Central Plaza Ste 307, Rome, GA 30161

www.TMPBooks.com

Publisher's Note

Estelle Herndon has been a client and friend since 2016, and I knew from the beginning that she and husband Robert have a special marriage.

Just over a year ago, she began sending me packets of love notes that Robert had written her, and she wanted to create a book with them. The notes are simple expressions of his love that he adds to that day's weather forecast; he has written her a note every day for more than 10 years.

Weatherly Love is a sampling of those notes, about a year's worth. As I transcribed them, the notes began speaking to me in a surprising way, and I realized that the notes were godly and passionate, like God's love for us, His children. We included scanned copies of a few of his notes, just for the reader's curiosity, and as an encouragement to be yourself in the notes you write to each other.

We've added Scripture verses to each note, and then a "Long Range" action plan to help couples strengthen and grow their own marriage.

The book is not a precise day-to-day set of 'homework,' nor is it laborious. Most of his notes were not dated, so we compiled them chronologically for a year, as best we knew to do, but it is not exact. You can start the book at any point in the year, but some of the notes mention major holidays, so we ordered them like the book starts in January.

We recommend grabbing a notebook or two (one for each of you) and use it to record anything suggested. Colored pencils or pens might be a great addition, too. We've created a Companion Notebook to make it easy, and to give you a keepsake after you've finished the book, but a standard notebook will also work. The notebooks are to share with each other as you go along, and then you'll give your notebook to your spouse at the end, as a memento of this journey.

We pray you'll find this book useful, insightful, and spiritual. May God use it to grow your marriage and your faith.

Thank you!

Tracy Ruckman

Publisher, TMP Books

Author's Note

Jesus is in the boat with Robert and me no matter how wild the storms in our lives become – He, our Lord, gives us peace as we journey together.

Loving well in life's storms. We may see happy days or not so happy days. We can experience cold, hot warm, humid times. Some sunshine, rain, clouds, fog, hail, snow, even lightning moments, even fire emotions. All are experiences in life as we grow.

We share with each other in love, in all its fullness as we live life.

The eyes of our Heavenly Father are on us, each and every day, paying close attention to our every movement as we travel through weatherly love. Our lives are joined together with Him as the center and remains with such unexpected, pure joy (James 1:2).

Pastor David Jeremiah said in one of his devotionals "The ups and downs of life may be God's way of teaching us to rely on Him. You can trust the rope of His grace."

This is ***Weatherly Love***, dear friends.

With Love,

Essie

Essie and Robert, wedding day

6am 57

10am 66

2pm 73

4pm 73

5pm 75

Rain this afternoon

Almost time to go. I am ready. You are doing so well at the ofc. You are one SPECIAL LADY. I love you and am so glad you are my wife. We are together on all things & forever. I love you. PTL our GOD who has/is blessed/blessing us so

RGW

I love Essie

5:00 AM	10:00 AM	2:00 PM	4:00 PM	5:00 PM
63	64	70	70	70

Rain.

New Year started.

So good starting it with you.

God is so good to you and me.

I love you – this year is already starting as one of our BEST because of the plans for the year 2021.

I love you.

I love being with you.

REH

"For I know the plans that I have for you,' declares the Lord,

'plans for prosperity and not for disaster,

to give you a future and a hope."

Jeremiah 29:11

LONG RANGE:

Set aside a few hours to set couple goals for the year. Goals could include creating or adding to a bucket list; household goals; financial goals; family goals; relationship goals; travel or vacation goals. Discuss personal goals, too, so you can support each other throughout the year.

5:00 AM	10:00 AM	2:00 PM	4:00 PM	5:00 PM
44	50	55	55	53

Cool all day. Sunshine in the afternoon.

Love just being with you even if it is at Belk's. You are what I need and desire. Whatever, whenever, just you!

I love you!

REH

"For your love is sweeter than wine."

Song of Solomon 1:2

LONG RANGE:

Recall the last time you were running errands or doing household chores together. Did you notice each other? Or do you take each other's presence for granted? What is one thing you can do to recognize each other, even in the mundane?

6:00 AM	10:00 AM	2:00 PM	4:00 PM	5:00 PM
39	48	62	63	62

This is the Lord's Day and Robert and Essie shall rejoice in it.

We love the Lord and each other.

God has been extremely good to you and me.

Love you.

REH

"This is the day which the Lord has made;

Let's rejoice and be glad in it."

Psalm 118:24

LONG RANGE:

How do you recognize the Lord's Day together?

5:00 AM	10:00 AM	2:00 PM	4:00 PM	5:00 PM
37	43	55	56	54

Trip in the making.

Let us keep doing this at least once a month.

Starting the year right.

I love you and just plain love being with you.

You crown the year with Your goodness,

And Your paths drip with abundance.

Psalm 65:11 (NKJV)

LONG RANGE:

Schedule an outing soon. This outing could be as simple and inexpensive as a picnic in the park, a day trip to explore a nearby town, or even a weekend getaway. Let the plan fit your budget and schedules but make it a fun getaway for the two of you.

6:00 AM	10:00 AM	2:00 PM	4:00 PM	5:00 PM
61	63	72	73	75

Sunny this afternoon.

I LOVE YOU!

You must know that by now.

You R my life. You R what keeps me going.

Love you.

Your BFF

REH

"A friend loves at all times."

Proverbs 17:17

LONG RANGE:

Is your spouse your BFF (Best Friend Forever)? If not, are you at least friends? How could you be a better friend to your spouse?

5:00 AM	10:00 AM	2:00 PM	4:00 PM	5:00 PM
52	64	77	78	76

Love was made for you and me.

I love you.

God loves us and has been so good to us.

You have been so good for me.

I love you.

REH

"See how great a love the Father has given us, that we would be called children of God."

1 John 3:1

LONG RANGE:

When was the last time you said, "I love you," to your spouse?

5:00 AM	10:00 AM	2:00 PM	4:00 PM	5:00 PM
60	59	64	63	61

Sunshine

Another week started. Soon another year will start.

All fine, all with you – just you and me.

Now, tomorrow, and always.

God shall keep us together under His love and protection.

He shall cover you with His feathers,

And under His wings you shall take refuge;

His truth shall be your shield and buckler.

Psalm 91:4 (NKJV)

LONG RANGE:

Build time into your weekly schedule for couple time. Time just to talk, unwind together, flirt with each other.

5:00 AM	10:00 AM	2:00 PM	4:00 PM	5:00 PM
73	81	86	86	82

Cooler today, plus rain.

Just love here today.

And it is overflowing to you.

Love. Love. Love.

"But now faith, hope, and love remain, these three; but the greatest of these is love."

1 Corinthians 13:13

LONG RANGE:

Does your love for each other overflow into all areas of your life?

5:00 AM	10:00 AM	2:00 PM	4:00 PM	5:00 PM
73	82	91	93	93

Hot!

Ten more days and you will be headed to the BEACH!

I love you and just love being with you, at the beach or at home or office, or anywhere.

I love you.

REH

"God is love,

and the one who remains in love remains in God,

and God remains in him."

1 John 4:16

LONG RANGE:

Do you have vacation or staycation plans this year? If so, discuss your plans and how to build some special couple time into it. If it's not doable this year, spend some time now talking out how to make one happen in the future. Where would you like to go? Dream a little together.

7:00 AM	10:00 AM	2:00 PM	4:00 PM	5:00 PM
72	81	91	91	90

Fog.

Got up at 6:40 am.

God is so good to us. PTL for you and me and our God that cares for us.

I love you!

REH

Humble yourselves under the mighty hand of God,

so that He may exalt you at the proper time,

having cast all your anxiety on Him,

because He cares about you.

1 Peter 5:6-7

LONG RANGE:

Make a list of reasons why you are thankful for your spouse, then share the lists with each other.

6:00 AM	10:00 AM	2:00 PM	4:00 PM	5:00 PM
68	81	90	90	90

I love you!

God has made us ONE and we shall so be forever as ONE.

I love you and really do just love BEING with you – WHEREVER.

Love,

REH

“For this reason a man shall leave his father and his mother,

and be joined to his wife;

and they shall become one flesh.”

Genesis 2:24

LONG RANGE:

Do you ever think of the two of you being ONE? How does this affect your decision-making and other areas of your life?

5:00 AM	10:00 AM	2:00 PM	4:00 PM	5:00 PM
75	81	81	84	88

Cloudy

Just love to you. More than you could imagine.

I love you!

REH

"You have enchanted my heart, my sister, my bride;

You have enchanted my heart …"

Song of Solomon 4:9

LONG RANGE:

Enchanted. Such a beautiful word. What does it mean to you? Have you ever felt enchanted?

6:00 AM	10:00 AM	2:00 PM	4:00 PM	5:00 PM
75	79	86	88	88

Love. Love. Love.

That is what it's all about.

Your love for me.

My love for you.

REH

"So husbands also ought to love their own wives as their own bodies.

He who loves his own wife loves himself."

Ephesians 5:28

LONG RANGE:

Discuss the Bible verse above. How does a husband love his wife as his own body?

6:00 AM	10:00 AM	2:00 PM	4:00 PM	5:00 PM
73	81	90	90	88

May rain 4, 5, 6 o'clock.

I LOVE YOU!

That is all that needs to be said.

It is so true!

REH

"Husbands, love your wives,

just as Christ also loved the church and gave Himself up for her …"

Ephesians 5:25

LONG RANGE:

How do you or could you give yourselves up for each other?

7:00 AM	10:00 AM	2:00 PM	4:00 PM	5:00 PM
70	70	73	73	72

*7 am note time

Cool today.

I'm up at 7 a.m.

Just love being with you. That satisfies me totally.

I love you.

REH.

"Who satisfies your years with good things,

So that your youth is renewed like the eagle."

Psalm 103:5

LONG RANGE:

Are you satisfied with the current state of your marriage? What could you do to make your marriage more satisfying for yourself and for each other?

5:00 AM	10:00 AM	2:00 PM	4:00 PM	5:00 PM
54	63	73	75	73

Sun in the afternoon.

I just plain love you, that's all there is to it.

It is a never-ending love.

You make me complete.

REH

"Love never ends."

1 Corinthians 13:8

(ESV)

LONG RANGE:

How has your love changed for your spouse since you first married? How do you see it changing in the coming years?

6:00 AM	10:00 AM	2:00 PM	4:00 PM	5:00 PM
55	64	81	82	81

Hot. Sunshine.

Woke up, took a shower first thing. Am doing OK.

I just love you

And

Love being with you.

REH

"We love, because He first loved us."

1 John 4:19

LONG RANGE:

Do you share your feelings with each other easily? Or is it difficult? Do you recognize different feelings in each other?

5:00 AM	10:00 AM	2:00 PM	4:00 PM	5:00 PM
48	54	59	61	57

Rain.

Cannot wait to move. So excited.

Just love you and love living life with you by my side.

God is awesome, too.

PTL.

I love you so much.

God is our source.

REH

"Although He was a Son, He learned obedience

from the things which He suffered.

And having been perfected,

He became the source

of eternal salvation for all those who obey Him."

Hebrews 5:8-9

LONG RANGE:

When was the last time you moved? Or are you moving soon? How did you / can you love each other well through the move?

5:00 AM	10:00 AM	2:00 PM	4:00 PM	5:00 PM
45	48	63	63	61

Nice today.

We are overloaded at present, but beautiful times are just ahead.

Trust God for everything.

I just love living life with you.

I love you.

REH

"In all your ways acknowledge Him,

And He will make your paths straight."

Proverbs 3:6

LONG RANGE:

Have you ever been overloaded with stress and responsibilities? How did you manage? What did your spouse do to help you through those times?

5:00 AM	10:00 AM	2:00 PM	4:00 PM	5:00 PM
30	45	61	61	59

Warmer today.

Starting another week with the one I love so much.

Life with you is just plain better.

I love you.

I love being with you.

REH

May the God of endurance and encouragement grant you to live
in such harmony with one another, in accord with Christ Jesus,
that together you may with one voice
glorify the God and Father of our Lord Jesus Christ.
Romans 15:5-6 (ESV)

LONG RANGE:

Do you live in harmony with one another? How can you improve?

5:00 AM	10:00 AM	2:00 PM	4:00 PM	5:00 PM
27	39	55	55	54

I am in love and love with you.

I love you more as I am with you more.

You are my life.

You are SPECIAL.

You are my BFF forever.

I love you.

REH

"How beautiful and how delightful you are,

My love, with all your delights!"

Song of Solomon 7:6

LONG RANGE:

Write love notes to each other, spelling out what makes your spouse so special.

5:00 AM	10:00 AM	2:00 PM	4:00 PM	5:00 PM
48	57	70	70	68

Nice today.

Now as time passes – my love increases.

Is there a limit?

I do not think so because it increases every day I am with you.

I love you.

REH

"May the Lord cause you to increase and overflow

in love for one another…"

1 Thessalonians 3:12

LONG RANGE:

How has your love increased for each other since you first met?

5:00 AM	10:00 AM	2:00 PM	3:00 PM	5:00 PM
57	61	66	68	66

Nice all day.

Let us worship the Lord, especially today for it is Sunday.

I love being with you on Sunday.

Actually, I love being with you any day and every day.

PTL for you.

God is good to us.

REH

"Come, let's worship and bow down,

Let's kneel before the Lord our Maker."

Psalm 95:6

LONG RANGE:

Do you feel comfortable worshiping God in front of your spouse? Why or why not? What's your favorite form of worship?

5:00 AM	10:00 AM	2:00 PM	4:00 PM	5:00 PM
64	57	61	61	57

Rain this morning. 5 am the warmest for the day.

Always remember you are SPECIAL, to GOD, to me, and many others.

You are BLESSED and you bless others.

I love you and always will.

REH

"Her children rise up and bless her;

Her husband also, and he praises her, saying:

'Many daughters have done nobly,

But you excel them all.'"

Proverbs 31:28

LONG RANGE:

When was the last time you noticed your spouse blessing you or someone else?

5:00 AM	10:00 AM	2:00 PM	4:00 PM	5:00 PM
43	52	66	66	64

Not as cold today.

Restful night – much needed and got.

I just love being with you.

As long as you are by my side, I am OK.

I love you.

REH

"I lay down and slept;

I awoke, for the Lord sustains me."

Psalm 3:5

LONG RANGE:

Do you set aside rest time? Could you provide some rest time for your spouse?

5:00 AM	10:00 AM	2:00 PM	4:00 PM	5:00 PM
55	57	61	61	61

Cool all day; rain this afternoon.

I love you and will always.

Enough said > you are my life.

PTL. PTL for you.

REH

"Praise the Lord!

Praise the Lord, my soul!

I will praise the Lord while I live;

I will sing praises to my God while I have my being."

Psalm 146:1-2

LONG RANGE:

What's your favorite praise and worship song?

5:00 AM	10:00 AM	2:00 PM	4:00 PM	5:00 PM
39	41	48	51	50

Cold all day, but sunshine, PTL.

Thursday already. Another week almost over.

Life is but a vapor.

So true so true.

Life with you is tops.

You, You, You – all I need.

Love you.

REH

"So teach us to number our days,

That we may present to You a heart of wisdom."

Psalm 90:12

LONG RANGE:

As time seems to pass faster the older we get, how can we make the most of our marriage?

5:00 AM	10:00 AM	2:00 PM	4:00 PM	5:00 PM
34	45	55	57	55

Cold all day, but sunshine most of day.

House is really coming along. Almost there, except for the new items.

Love you getting your house like you want it.

You deserve so much more than you are getting.

I love you and love taking care of you.

REH

"Husbands, love your wives, just as Christ also loved the church and gave Himself up for her, so that He might sanctify her, having cleansed her by the washing of water with the word, that He might present to Himself the church in all her glory, having no spot or wrinkle or any such thing; but that she would be holy and blameless."

Ephesians 5:25-27

LONG RANGE:

What are some ways you can help take better care of your spouse?

5:00 AM	10:00 AM	2:00 PM	4:00 PM	5:00 PM
37	45	50	48	46

Much colder today.

Love you so.

It is exciting now but also difficult with moving. I just can't wait to get to our new office.

Love you and love you being with me everywhere.

God is good to us.

PTL.

I love you.

REH

"The Lord is good,

A stronghold in the day of trouble,

And He knows those who take refuge in Him."

Nahum 1:7

LONG RANGE:

What are some exciting changes happening in your life (or that happened recently)? Give thanks to God together for His goodness in your lives.

5:00 AM	10:00 AM	2:00 PM	4:00 PM	5:00 PM
36	43	55	55	54

Much like yesterday.

Our God is our Rock.

I love you and we will be all right.

God be for you, who can be against you?

I love you.

I love being with you.

REH

"If God is for us, who can be against us?"

Romans 8:31
(ESV)

LONG RANGE:

How has God been a Rock for you recently?

5:00 AM	10:00 AM	2:00 PM	4:00 PM	5:00 PM
45	50	59	61	57

Move time will be here before you know it.

Time goes so fast. Life is but a vapor.

Life with you is awesome.

Just to be with you is my desire.

I love you.

God is our God and so good to us.

REH

"Yet you do not know what your life will be like tomorrow.

For you are just a vapor that appears for a little while, and then vanishes away."

James 4:14

LONG RANGE:

What is your greatest desire for your marriage?

5:00 AM	10:00 AM	2:00 PM	4:00 PM	5:00 PM
39	46	57	59	57

Cold ALL Day.

Start the work week with the one you love, and you will find it is not work – but pleasure.

It is always pleasurable being with the one you love.

I love you.

REH

Jesus said,

"I came so that they would have life,

and have it abundantly."

John 10:10

LONG RANGE:

Share something pleasant that happened during your work week.

5:00 AM	10:00 AM	2:00 PM	4:00 PM	5:00 PM
61	59	66	66	64

May rain at 4 p.m.

Just love here for you.

And it is a whole lot of love. All I have is love for Essie.

You are SPECIAL in many eyes – especially MINE.

We are partners-in-life.

Love you.

REH

"In addition to all these things put on love,

which is the perfect bond of unity."

Colossians 3:14

LONG RANGE:

Do each of you carry an equal load in your marriage? If one of you feels overloaded in an area, how can the other partner with you to help?

5:00 AM	10:00 AM	2:00 PM	4:00 PM	5:00 PM
48	46	54	54	52

Cool all day; sunshine.

Christmas decorations stored. Another season is starting. As long as it is with you, I am OK.

I love you and love being with you.

You make me complete.

I love you.

REH

Arise, shine;

For your light has come!

And the glory of the Lord is risen upon you.

Isaiah 60:1 (NKJV)

LONG RANGE:

What will be your favorite memory from this past Christmas season?

On the Cross

As I stand here
Looking deep into the eyes before me
I see a desire to live ...

I see love ...
I see tenderness ...
I see compassion ...

I also see what your eyes have seen ...

The pain
The sadness
The tears

I ask ...
What have you learned?

The answer I receive is ...
"To believe in the eyes before you, for they are
The answer."

Through those eyes I see the answer
Everyday in people like you ...

Who help guide us
Build us ...
Love us ...
So that we may one day rejoice
Before the great "I AM."

Robert E. Herndon ©

5:00 AM	10:00 AM	2:00 PM	4:00 PM	5:00 PM
73	84	93	93	91

I love you.

Want you to go to church with me this morning. Of course, I'm talking about church upstairs.*

God is so good to us.

We must keep on serving and loving God and others.

I love you.

REH

*Editor's Note: Some of these notes were written while quarantined during the pandemic in 2020 and 2021.

"Beloved, if God so loved us, we also ought to love one another."

1 John 4:11

LONG RANGE:

How has the pandemic changed your marriage? Has it made it better or worse? What changes should you make to protect and grow your relationship for the future?

5:00 AM	10:00 AM	2:00 PM	4:00 PM	5:00 PM
75	84	93	93	93

Boy Day Today

Me and the Boy will do whatever.

See you at the office for breakfast.

I love you.

You are my dream girl.

No one is like you.

Love to you.

REH

"'My dove, in the clefts of the rock,

In the hiding place of the mountain pathway,

Let me see how you look,

Let me hear your voice;

For your voice is pleasant,

And you look delightful.'"

Song of Solomon 2:14

LONG RANGE:

When was the last time you ate breakfast together? Plan to cook breakfast together this week – even if it's breakfast for dinner.

5:00 AM	10:00 AM	2:00 PM	4:00 PM	5:00 PM
73	82	91	91	90

We both had a good day yesterday with 'the boy.'

Days are always good when you are present.

I love you now and always will.

I love you, Essie.

REH

Oh give thanks to the Lord, for he is good,

for his steadfast love endures forever!

Psalm 107:1

(ESV)

LONG RANGE:

What is the longest time you've ever spent apart since you've been married? How did that time apart make you feel?

Another Note
That says
I love you!
U Make Me Complete.
REH

5:00 AM	10:00 AM	2:00 PM	4:00 PM	5:00 PM
72	81	88	90	90

Warmer today.

God has blessed you (and us) greatly.

You are His servant, and you are reaping rewards.

I love you, servant of the Most High God.

REH

"This is the way any person is to regard us:

as servants of Christ

and stewards of the mysteries of God."

1 Corinthians 4:1

LONG RANGE:

How do you serve God individually? As a couple? What's one thing you could do to serve Him more?

5:00 AM	10:00 AM	2:00 PM	4:00 PM	5:00 PM
64	75	82	82	82

Forgiveness and mercy are just like love, they cover multiple transgressions.

I ask you to FORGIVE me and have MERCY on me.

You are my ONLY DESIRE to keep living. You are my BBF forever. You are my life.

Most of all, I sinned against our God, who is with us and protects us daily.

Thanks that God has unconditional LOVE.

PTL for you and God in my life.

I love you.

REH

So, as those who have been chosen of God, holy and beloved,

put on a heart of compassion, kindness, humility, gentleness, and patience;

bearing with one another, and forgiving each other,

whoever has a complaint against anyone;

just as the Lord forgave you, so must you do also.

In addition to all these things put on love, which is the perfect bond of unity.

Colossians 3:12-14

LONG RANGE:

Is it hard for you to ask for forgiveness when you've done something wrong? Summon the courage to ask your spouse for forgiveness today.

5:00 AM	10:00 AM	2:00 PM	4:00 PM	5:00 PM
67	69	68	67	65

Your light shines as you pray for others.

U R a true prayer warrior.

I love you.

I love the way you are.

Would you consider being my Valentine?

REH

Jesus said,

"Let your light so shine before men,

that they may see your good works

and glorify your Father in heaven."

Matthew 5:16 (NKJV)

LONG RANGE:

How does your spouse's light shine for Jesus?

To Essie,

I swear under penalty of perjury that I had a V-Day card for you,

but I cannot find it. It must be at home.

However, I can write you a card from my heart.

You are my VALENTINE and ALWAYS WILL BE.

You make my life complete.

I love living life with you, our work, our family, our home, our church,

our everything.

I am IN LOVE WITH YOU. You bring out the best in me.

Our dreams together will materialize because of the God we serve.

We are ONE as God ordained us to be.

Together, with God, we can do anything and all things to honor God

and our lives.

You are the reason for me wanting to live.

I love being with you, anywhere, or doing whatever. If I am with you,

I am pleased.

You are my Valentine, but you are also my life.

I love you.

REH

5:00 AM	10:00 AM	2:00 PM	4:00 PM	5:00 PM
39	52	66	66	64

Essie,

You are my heart.

REH

LONG RANGE:

Write and/or draw a Valentine Love Letter or Poem to your spouse.

5:00 AM	10:00 AM	2:00 PM	4:00 PM	5:00 PM
54	63	75	81	81

Sunshine.

Good day for Valentine's Day.

You R my Valentine.

You are my Sunshine.

You are my all.

You are my life.

God has blessed us so we shall honor and praise our God.

Amen.

I love you.

REH

With my whole heart I have sought You;

Oh, let me not wander from Your commandments!

Psalm 119:10 (NKJV)

LONG RANGE:

Romance your spouse.

5:00 AM	10:00 AM	2:00 PM	4:00 PM	5:00 PM
72	79	84	82	82

Rain – 40% chance.

Church today, either 9:30 or 11. I do not know which.

But I do know I LOVE YOU.

REH

Jesus said,

"For where two or three have gathered together in My name, I am there in their midst."

Matthew 18:20

LONG RANGE:

Do you and your spouse pray together?

5:00 AM	10:00 AM	2:00 PM	4:00 PM	5:00 PM
61	70	75	79	79

Not as hot today.

Love being with you anywhere – just as long as YOU R THERE!

I love you.

REH

Nevertheless we, according to His promise,

look for new heavens and a new earth in which righteousness dwells.

2 Peter 3:13 (NKJV)

LONG RANGE:

Do you have a favorite "happy place" together as a couple?

5:00 AM	10:00 AM	2:00 PM	4:00 PM	5:00 PM
66	79	88	90	88

Sunny, and then partly cloudy.

Just a little note that carries BIG love for you.

You are my life.

I love you.

REH

Beloved, let's love one another; for love is from God,

and everyone who loves has been born of God and knows God.

1 John 4:7

LONG RANGE:

Send your spouse a short love note this week.

5:00 AM	10:00 AM	2:00 PM	4:00 PM	5:00 PM
75	79	90	91	90

Hot.

Just love for you this morning.

Love covers all wrongs.

I love you and

I love just being with you.

Beach in near future, OK?

REH

Above all, keep fervent in your love for one another,

because love covers a multitude of sins.

1 Peter 4:8

LONG RANGE:

Plan something fun together for a future date.

5:00 AM	10:00 AM	2:00 PM	4:00 PM	5:00 PM
72	81	88	86	84

Cloudy. 60/70% chance of RAIN.

Must be BEACH TIME somewhere in our future.

Oh, well – you know what? Just being with you is what really matters.

Beach, house, or office, or church, or wherever, just to be with you is what I want.

REH

You have made known to me the ways of life;

You will make me full of joy in Your presence.

Acts 2:28 (NKJV)

LONG RANGE:

Share your favorite memory of your togetherness with each other. What makes that memory your favorite?

5:00 AM	10:00 AM	2:00 PM	4:00 PM	5:00 PM
72	79	88	88	88

Fog and Rain. Oh! What a wonderful day!

Your work is awesome.

You are due a big reward.

We will see what God has in store for you.

You sincerely deserve it.

You are WONDERFUL and a PLEASURE just to be around you,

Here, office, or wherever.

I love YOU!

REH

Whatever you do, work heartily, as for the Lord and not for men,

knowing that from the Lord you will receive the inheritance as your reward.

You are serving the Lord Christ.

Colossians 3:23-24

LONG RANGE:

Praise your spouse for something they've done well recently.

5:00 AM	10:00 AM	2:00 PM	4:00 PM	5:00 PM
55	56	63	65	63

Much cooler.

It's all about LOVE.

We have it.

We love it.

We are ONE in God's spirit and ways.

Let us continue.

LOVE LOVE LOVE.

REH

For by one Spirit we were all baptized into one body,

whether Jews or Greeks, whether slaves or free,

and we were all made to drink of one Spirit.

1 Corinthians 12:13

LONG RANGE:

Recall a time when you realized the two of you were acting as one. Does this come naturally, or does it take effort?

6:00 AM	10:00 AM	2:00 PM	4:00 PM	5:00 PM
57	61	70	72	72

Cool all day.

You must stay close to me.

We will keep each other warm with our love.

REH

For lo, the winter is past,

The rain is over and gone.

The flowers appear on the earth;

The time of singing has come,

And the voice of the turtledove

Is heard in our land.

Song of Solomon 2:11-12 (NKJV)

LONG RANGE:

Settle in for a night of movies and snuggle time.

6:00 AM	10:00 AM	2:00 PM	4:00 PM	5:00 PM
48	59	72	75	75

Warmer. Sunshine day.

Love rules in our lives.

As long as we stay under God's guidance, we shall be safe and sound.

I love you and love being beside you at all times.

REH

And the Lord will continually guide you,

And satisfy your desire in scorched places,

And give strength to your bones;

And you will be like a watered garden,

And like a spring of water whose waters do not fail.

Isaiah 58:11

LONG RANGE:

When was the last time you asked God for His guidance in a situation? What was the outcome?

5:00 AM	10:00 AM	2:00 PM	4:00 PM	5:00 PM
73	81	90	91	90

Hot.

You can tell you R better.

PTL PTL

Your meds from doctor must be working.

I love you.

We are one in sickness or in health, up or down, or whatever.

It is US TOGETHER.

I love you.

REH

Praise the Lord!

Praise God in His sanctuary;

Praise Him in His mighty expanse.

Praise Him for His mighty deeds;

Praise Him according to His excellent greatness.

Psalm 150:1-2

LONG RANGE:

Do you have contingency plans should one of you get sick for an extended period? Discuss the "what-ifs" and develop a plan.

5:00 AM	10:00 AM	2:00 PM	4:00 PM	5:00 PM
75	82	91	93	91

Thanks for your note.

I, as am able, will always take care of you.

You are my LOVE, my Life, my Wife.

I want to take good care of you.

We are ONE!

I love you!

REH

You husbands in the same way, live with your wives in an understanding way,
as with someone weaker, since she is a woman;
and show her honor as a fellow heir of the grace of life,
so that your prayers will not be hindered.
1 Peter 3:7

LONG RANGE:

Write a love note to your spouse, focusing on ways you want to take care of him/her.

5:00 AM	10:00 AM	2:00 PM	4:00 PM	5:00 PM
62	57	66	66	70

Cooler today.

Shelter-in-place is a good prelude for how we can slow down our office work.

God is so good to us.

I love you.

I love being with you, even if it is shelter-in-place.

I love Essie.

REH

One who dwells in the shelter of the Most High

Will lodge in the shadow of the Almighty.

Psalm 91:1

LONG RANGE:

Could your marriage benefit from a slower pace? What are some ways you might implement that into your schedules?

5:00 AM	10:00 AM	2:00 PM	4:00 PM	5:00 PM
43	54	70	73	75

Sunshine all day!

Warmer.

The Rule

"Let Love Rule."

The Rule is operating in our lives with us.

Let it be so forever and ever.

I love you.

REH

Let all that you do be done in love.

1 Corinthians 16:14

LONG RANGE:

Does love always rule in your marriage? How could that improve?

5:00 AM	10:00 AM	2:00 PM	4:00 PM	5:00 PM
70	77	86	88	88

Much better for me.

Much better for you.

PTL for us both.

I love you.

See you at church at 8 a.m.

Love to Essie.

REH

Bless the Lord, O my soul,

and all that is within me,

bless his holy name!

Psalm 103:1

(ESV)

LONG RANGE:

Give thanks to God for some recent blessings in your lives.

5:00 AM	10:00 AM	2:00 PM	4:00 PM	5:00 PM
77	79	86	88	88

Do hope you are much better.

I believe you will be.

I just love you.

You must always remain at my side.

I have got to be with you – WHEREVER.

REH

For I am confident of this very thing,

that He who began a good work among you

will complete it by the day of Christ Jesus.

Philippians 1:6

LONG RANGE:

How has your spouse grown (mentally, emotionally, spiritually) since you married?

5:00 AM	10:00 AM	2:00 PM	4:00 PM	5:00 PM
72	79	82	84	84

Cloudy.

Another week at work over.

Just as long as you are with me, it is all alright.

You and you only, that is what counts on earth.

I love you.

I love being with you.

REH

Then the Lord God said,

"It is not good for the man to be alone;

I will make him a helper suitable for him."

Genesis 2:18

LONG RANGE:

What do you like most about being married? What do you like least?

5:00 AM	10:00 AM	2:00 PM	4:00 PM	5:00 PM
70	75	82	81	79

Fog, morning rain. Cooling in the evening.

I just love you.

LOVE LOVE LOVE is all I can say about you.

You make my day.

You make my night.

You make my everything.

REH

"We will rejoice in you and be joyful;

We will praise your love more than wine.

Rightly do they love you."

Song of Solomon 1:4

LONG RANGE:

When did you first realize you were in love with your spouse? What do you love most about him/her?

5:00 AM	10:00 AM	2:00 PM	4:00 PM	5:00 PM
75	79	90	90	90

Warmer today.

I want to go somewhere.

Maybe anywhere, with just YOU and ME.

I love you.

REH

And Jesus said to them,

"Go into all the world and preach the gospel to all creation."

Mark 16:15

LONG RANGE:

If you could, where would you go today?

5:00 AM	10:00 AM	2:00 PM	4:00 PM	5:00 PM
73	75	82	84	84

May rain in the afternoon.

I LOVE YOU!

That is it. That's what counts.

I love you.

REH

"What kind of beloved is your beloved,

O most beautiful among women?

What kind of beloved is your beloved,

That you make us swear in this way?"

Song of Solomon 5:9

LONG RANGE:

Make a plan for the next rainy day to take a walk together in the rain, snuggling under a single umbrella, listening to the sounds of nature around you as you walk.

5:00 AM	10:00 AM	2:00 PM	4:00 PM	5:00 PM
66	75	88	88	88

As long as I am with you, the holiday is great, even if we are at home.

Just being with you is what matters.

I love you.

I love being with you.

LOVE LOVE LOVE TO YOU.

REH

"In the house of the righteous there is much treasure …"

Proverbs 15:6

LONG RANGE:

What makes your home most special to you?

5:00 AM	10:00 AM	2:00 PM	4:00 PM	5:00 PM
72	79	88	90	90

Start the work week with love.

That's you and me,

You and me, forever,

Together.

One couple – one God.

I love you and I thank God for you.

PTL.

REH

I thank my God always concerning you

for the grace of God which was given you in Christ Jesus.

1 Corinthians 1:4

LONG RANGE:

Do your weekly routines bring you together as a couple? Or do they create conflict and need some adjusting?

5:00 AM	10:00 AM	2:00 PM	4:00 PM	5:00 PM
66	77	88	90	90

Let's go to church upstairs at 9:30 a.m.

Let's continue to love each other as we do now.

Let's honor God as we move along life's path.

I love you and I want you by my side always.

REH

For you have been bought for a price:

therefore glorify God in your body.

1 Corinthians 6:20

LONG RANGE:

What are some ways you can honor God as a couple this week?

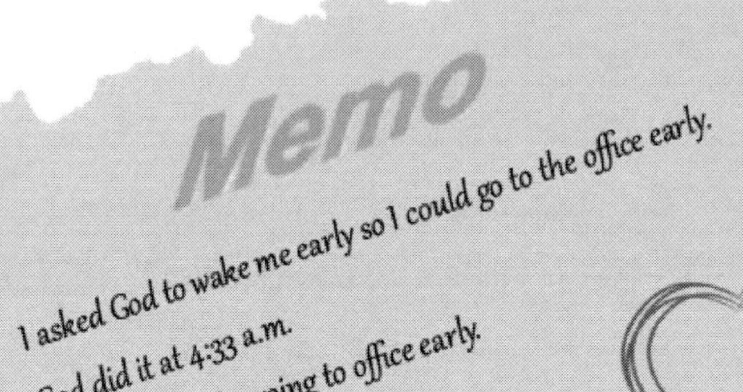
Memo
I asked God to wake me early so I could go to the office early.
God did it at 4:33 a.m.
REH did obey by going to office early.
Leaving home at 8 a.m.
Love to you.
Forever and ever.
From me, REH

5:00 AM	10:00 AM	2:00 PM	4:00 PM	5:00 PM
66	77	88	88	88

Partly cloudy.

Bloodwork today. Doctor Friday for both.

I love you.

Shelter-in-place is not so bad if you are with the right person, like I am.

Just being with you doing whatever or nothing is OK with me.

REH

And Jesus said to them,
"Come away by yourselves to a secluded place
and rest a little while."
Mark 6:31

LONG RANGE:

Are you facing some challenges individually or as a couple? Discuss ways you can weather them.

5:00 AM	10:00 AM	2:00 PM	4:00 PM	5:00 PM
63	72	82	84	84

Very warm. "Hot."

Can't believe it's Thursday.

Time goes so fast.

I am glad it is with you that I spent my time with.

I LOVE YOU!

REH

And we know that God causes all things to work together for good

to those who love God,

to those who are called according to His purpose.

Romans 8:28

LONG RANGE:

Recall the last time something challenging that worked out for the good for one or both of you.

5:00 AM	10:00 AM	2:00 PM	4:00 PM	5:00 PM
70	75	79	79	79

Not as warm as yesterday.

Love from me just overflows to you.

It is non-stop and unlimited.

It will never run out.

I LOVE YOU.

REH

You prepare a table before me

in the presence of my enemies;

you anoint my head with oil;

my cup overflows.

Psalm 23:5

LONG RANGE:

Are you feeling empty or drained? What's one way your spouse can help you refill and refresh?

5:00 AM	10:00 AM	2:00 PM	4:00 PM	5:00 PM
70	75	84	88	86

I am IN LOVE with you still …

More than when we first started going together.

Remember Lake Henry?

Love much much more now – because it increases as each day passes

My love for you.

But the fruit of the Spirit is love, joy, peace, longsuffering, kindness,

goodness, faithfulness, gentleness, self-control.

Galatians 5:22-23

(NKJV)

LONG RANGE:

How long have you been in love? How long has it been since you "felt in love"? Schedule a date to rekindle that romance.

5:00 AM	10:00 AM	2:00 PM	4:00 PM	5:00 PM
68	75	88	90	90

Summer weather.

I just love you so.

You R my life.

You R what keeps me going.

I love you.

REH

I press on toward the goal for the prize

of the upward call of God in Christ Jesus.

Philippians 3:14

LONG RANGE:

How does your spouse help keep you going? How could he/she do something more?

5:00 AM	10:00 AM	2:00 PM	4:00 PM	5:00 PM
64	77	88	90	90

Partly cloudy; fog.

Mark it in your book that REH just loves you more and more as each day passes.

It will always be like that.

I love you!

REH

"The one who overcomes will be clothed the same way,
in white garments; and I will not erase his name from the book of life,
and I will confess his name before My Father and before His angels."
Revelation 3:5

LONG RANGE:

Name something that you've overcome as a couple and celebrate the victory together.

5:00 AM	10:00 AM	2:00 PM	4:00 PM	5:00 PM
61	72	82	84	86

Wow, I had a note this morning from my BFF!

This is a note back to you WITH LOVE

Nothing but LOVE and just for YOU.

REH

Because your steadfast love is better than life,

my lips will praise you.

Psalm 63:3

LONG RANGE:

Write a sweet or funny love note to your spouse.

6:00 AM	10:00 AM	2:00 PM	4:00 PM	5:00 PM
54	63	75	81	81

Sunshine.

You are my sunshine.

You are my all.

You are my life.

God has blessed us so we shall honor and praise our God.

Amen.

I love you!

REH

Blessed be the God and Father of our Lord Jesus Christ,

who has blessed us with every spiritual blessing

in the heavenly places in Christ.

Ephesians 1:3

LONG RANGE:

Spend some time together in the sunshine. Take a walk or hike, go for a drive, explore a flea market or enjoy picnic in the park.

5:00 AM	10:00 AM	2:00 PM	4:00 PM	5:00 PM
53	55	67	70	70

Sunshine at 2 p.m. Cooler today.

We will go to church tonite – upstairs at 7 p.m.

I love going to church with you.

Come to think of it, I love going ANYWHERE with you.

Why? 'Cause I love you!

REH

I was glad when they said to me,

"Let's go to the house of the Lord."

Psalm 122:1

LONG RANGE:

Are you active in church? Or do you hold church at home? Discuss your thoughts and hopes and feelings about church as a whole, personally and as a couple.

5:00 AM	10:00 AM	2:00 PM	4:00 PM	5:00 PM
54	61	73	73	72

Warmer today. Cloudy.

Our God will prevail.

You and I are in God's hands.

I just love being where you are. I love you.

So glad you are getting better each day.

I love you.

REH

The Lord reigns, He is clothed with majesty;

The Lord has clothed and encircled Himself with strength.

Indeed, the world is firmly established; it will not be moved.

Psalm 93:1

LONG RANGE:

What does it mean to you to be in God's hands?

5:00 AM	10:00 AM	2:00 PM	4:00 PM	5:00 PM
39	52	64	64	63

Cool all day.

Need a new patch on this morning.

I just love how you take care of me.

I just plain love you.

I love everything about you.

You make me a better person.

LOVE, LOVE to you, my BFF.

REH

Strength and dignity are her clothing,

And she smiles at the future.

She opens her mouth in wisdom,

And the teaching of kindness is on her tongue.

She watches over the activities of her household,

And does not eat the bread of idleness.

Proverbs 31:25-27

LONG RANGE:

How does your spouse make you a better person?

5:00 AM	10:00 AM	2:00 PM	4:00 PM	5:00 PM
72	81	88	90	88

May rain this afternoon. 50% chance.

Now you can say START PACKING.

Yes, it is time for us to get ready to go.

I love you and cannot wait till we shelter at the beach.

With you is all that matters.

Let us go pack.

REH

Jesus said,

"Come to Me, all who are weary and burdened, and I will give you rest."

Matthew 11:28

LONG RANGE:

When you squeeze in a vacation, do you like going to new places or returning to somewhere familiar?

5:00 AM	10:00 AM	2:00 PM	4:00 PM	5:00 PM
72	81	90	91	91

Start packing.

Time is near.

Beach, here we come.

You and I can shelter-in-place but at a different place.

We both must take care of ourselves.

I love you and want you with me always.

REH

If you abide in me, and my words abide in you,

ask whatever you wish, and it will be done for you.

John 15:7

LONG RANGE:

What does it mean for the Lord to abide in you?

5:00 AM	10:00 AM	2:00 PM	4:00 PM	5:00 PM
73	82	93	95	97

Almost 100!

Sunday – Lord's Day.

Really, every day is the Lord's Day.

Without God, we have no day.

I love you.

I love just being with you, wherever, whatever.

Okay?

REH

There remains a Sabbath rest for the people of God.

For the one who has entered His rest has himself also rested from his works,

as God did from His.

Hebrews 4:9-10

LONG RANGE:

If you recognize the Sabbath, what's your favorite aspect? If you don't, discuss ways you might start.

5:00 AM	10:00 AM	2:00 PM	4:00 PM	5:00 PM
70	81	90	93	93

Whatever is wrong with me – it is ME – no one else.

I will take it to the Lord:

"where does my help come from? The Lord, who made Earth and Heaven."

You are the most POSITIVE, good, Christian, Christ-serving person I know.

Keep up with yourself just as you are, because you are the right way.

It is ME that is wrong.

I love you.

REH

If we confess our sins, He is faithful and righteous,

so that He will forgive us our sins and

cleanse us from all unrighteousness.

1 John 1:9

LONG RANGE:

Are you able to admit when you are wrong? Is there anything you need to confess to God or to your spouse and ask for forgiveness?

6 am 55
10 am 63
2 pm 72
4 pm 73
5 pm 73

There is so much good things to say about you, that I never run out of good things to say. You are very SPECIAL. You are a Servant of the Most High God. What else needs to be said? I Love you and Love the way you are to me.

PTL our God - we will attend WORSHIP this morning

[signature]

5:00 AM	10:00 AM	2:00 PM	4:00 PM	5:00 PM
77	84	93	95	95

Starting at 77. Hot.

Will be hot today.

Really, it is always hot when you are around.

Get it?

You R "HOT" looking.

I love you.

REH

"You are altogether beautiful, my darling,

And there is no blemish on you."

Song of Solomon 4:7

LONG RANGE:

Do you build each other up with your words and actions? Or do you chip away at each other with criticism?

5:00 AM	10:00 AM	2:00 PM	4:00 PM	5:00 PM
73	82	88	88	88

More hot today. Rain afternoon.

Hope you are feeling much better this morning.

You are my Sunshine and my feel good person.

You down, me down.

You up, me up.

I love you and will always.

REH

For I will pour water on the thirsty land,
and streams on the dry ground;
I will pour my Spirit upon your offspring,
and my blessing on your descendants.
Isaiah 44:3 (ESV)

LONG RANGE:

How does your spouse's mood affect your own?

5:00 AM	10:00 AM	2:00 PM	4:00 PM	5:00 PM
73	82	91	91	91

Another work week passed.

Seems so fast.

I just love you and just love being with you.

We do not have to be doing anything, but loving each other.

REH

O God, you are my God; earnestly I seek you;

my soul thirsts for you;

my flesh faints for you,

as in a dry and weary land where there is no water.

Psalm 63:1 (ESV)

LONG RANGE:

Plan a restful day together.

5:00 AM	10:00 AM	2:00 PM	4:00 PM	5:00 PM
75	84	91	93	93

Decision made.

Beach, here we come.

We will be safe.

We will enjoy.

We will take care of ourselves.

We will praise God.

We will love each other.

We will love the trip.

REH

Delight yourself in the Lord,

and he will give you the desires of your heart.

Psalm 37:4

LONG RANGE:

Some decisions are easy to make, others not so much. Spend some time discussing and praying about some decisions you're currently facing.

5:00 AM	10:00 AM	2:00 PM	4:00 PM	5:00 PM
72	84	91	93	93

Hot.

Love here for you, you only, the kind of love I am talking about.

Just being with you makes me content.

REH

But godliness with contentment is great gain,

for we brought nothing into the world,

and we cannot take anything out of the world.

1 Timothy 6:6-7 (ESV)

LONG RANGE:

How does the word 'contentment' make you feel? Are you content with your life? Which aspects are you most contented with? Least?

5:00 AM	10:00 AM	2:00 PM	4:00 PM	5:00 PM
73	82	91	93	93

As you think of others, we have no problems.

We are blessed by God and we shall continue to trust and serve God.

We are ONE as God has made us.

May we Praise the Lord.

I love you and always will.

REH

He who finds a wife finds a good thing

and obtains favor from the Lord.

Proverbs 18:22 (ESV)

LONG RANGE:

Name a specific way that God has blessed you as a couple.

5:00 AM	10:00 AM	2:00 PM	4:00 PM	5:00 PM
72	82	91	93	93

Beach time near.

Really, it does not make a difference to me.

Just so I am with you – wherever it may be – that is what counts.

REH

I love you!

A generous person will be prosperous,

And one who gives others plenty of water will himself be given plenty.

Proverbs 11:25

LONG RANGE:

Do you prefer beach, mountains, lakes, desert, or plains?

5:00 AM	10:00 AM	2:00 PM	4:00 PM	5:00 PM
75	84	93	93	93

Things happen, some good, some not so good.

However, God is Supreme.

My love for you is locked in.

We are together whether things are good or not so good.

God is always Good to us.

PTL.

I love you.

REH

Consider it all joy, my brothers and sisters, when you encounter various trials,

knowing that the testing of your faith produces endurance.

James 1:2-3

LONG RANGE:

When you face trials, what helps you get through them the most? How can you help each other get through the difficulties of life?

5:00 AM	10:00 AM	2:00 PM	4:00 PM	5:00 PM
73	84	93	95	95

One week from today BEACH, here we come.

I love you whether we are at the beach or home or office or anywhere.

I love you.

REH

I know that there is nothing better for them

than to rejoice and to do good in one's lifetime;

moreover, that every person who eats and drinks sees good in all his labor—

this is the gift of God.

Ecclesiastes 3:12-13

LONG RANGE:

Is it hard for you to relax or wind down? Do you have a place in your home or a favorite vacation spot that gives you resting space?

5:00 AM	10:00 AM	2:00 PM	4:00 PM	5:00 PM
70	79	88	90	90

Cloudy.

I love you.

All I do is try to take care of you.

I want you with me forever and ever.

Because I love you.

REH

Peace I leave with you; my peace I give to you.

Not as the world gives do I give to you.

Let not your hearts be troubled, neither let them be afraid.

John 14:27 (ESV)

LONG RANGE:

What does forever look like to you?

5:00 AM	10:00 AM	2:00 PM	4:00 PM	5:00 PM
73	84	93	93	93

The time is now.

Let us go to the beach.

I love you and just plain love being with you – wherever.

REH

Rejoice in the Lord always; again I will say, rejoice.

Philippians 4:4 (ESV)

LONG RANGE:

What's your beach preference? Gentle waves and a book; pounding surf and a board (surf or boogie); or lots of shells to gather?

6am 63

10am 66

2pm 73 — Not as hot as yesterday

4pm 75

5pm 75

Another day with a
beautiful woman by my
side. Life is great for
me. You make it that
way. I love you and I
will always Love you.

PTL our God who blesses
you + I every day

[illegible]

LOVE YOU

=

5:00 AM	10:00 AM	2:00 PM	4:00 PM	5:00 PM
73	79	82	86	82

Rain.

You do an awesome job of helping people.

I am so proud of you.

You cannot be replaced.

I love you.

I love just being with you.

REH

Do nothing from selfishness or empty conceit, but with humility
consider one another as more important than yourselves;
do not merely look out for your own personal interests,
but also for the interests of others.
Philippians 2:3-4

LONG RANGE:

Brag on your spouse, to his/her face right now, and later, to others.

5:00 AM	10:00 AM	2:00 PM	4:00 PM	5:00 PM
73	79	86	88	88

Cloudy. Rain @ 4 p.m.

One week. One day.

Our beach decision must be made.

As long as I am with you (wherever) is good enough for me.

But, I do like the beach.

I love you!

REH

I will instruct you and teach you in the way which you should go;

I will advise you with My eye upon you.

Psalm 32:8

LONG RANGE:

Do each of you have equal say in decisions made for your family? Is one of you more of the decision-maker than the other? Does this work well for you both, or do adjustments need to be made?

5:00 AM	10:00 AM	2:00 PM	4:00 PM	5:00 PM
73	81	91	93	93

PTL we are home.

Great time, but there is no place like home.

I love just being with you – wherever.

We just have to love and serve God greatly because God has blessed us so greatly. Amen.

God above all!

REH

By wisdom a house is built,

And by understanding it is established;

4 And by knowledge the rooms are filled

With all precious and pleasant riches.

Proverbs 24:3-4

LONG RANGE:

Is your home a haven? A safe retreat from the world? If not, how could you make it more so? If it is, share what you love most about that aspect.

5:00 AM	10:00 AM	2:00 PM	4:00 PM	5:00 PM
48	59	70	72	73

Warmer than yesterday.

Today is the day that makes Christianity different than all other religions.

He has RISEN.

PTL, PTL, PTL.

We, too, will rise.

Love you.

REH

The angel said to the women, "Do not be afraid;

for I know that you are looking for Jesus who has been crucified.

He is not here, for He has risen, just as He said.

Come, see the place where He was lying.

And go quickly and tell His disciples that He has risen from the dead."

Matthew 28:5-7

LONG RANGE:

Remember your first Easter together. Have you created any Easter traditions during your marriage?

5:00 AM	10:00 AM	2:00 PM	4:00 PM	5:00 PM
64	73	84	86	88

Do whatever is necessary to get your teeth right.

Teeth (their health) affects your overall health. They must be correct.

I love you, still & more, and I have been with you for over half a century.

It has been wonderful just to have you by my side.

Love you.

REH

Long life is in her right hand;

In her left hand are riches and honor.

Proverbs 3:16

LONG RANGE:

Do you have individual health goals? Share them with each other and then support each other's goals.

5:00 AM	10:00 AM	2:00 PM	4:00 PM	5:00 PM
66	68	78	77	75

Love does rule.

Love does cover over many, many transgressions.

Love is our rule.

I love you and you love me and we will love each other forever.

PTL for you and my life.

REH

I love you.

For God so loved the world that He gave His only begotten Son,

that whoever believes in Him should not perish but have everlasting life.

John 3:16

LONG RANGE:

Is it hard to forgive each other? Or do you forgive easily?

5:00 AM	10:00 AM	2:00 PM	4:00 PM	5:00 PM
66	73	86	88	88

Another week starting.

Another week with the one I love the most here on Earth.

God has been good to you and me.

Let us PTL for our lives.

I love you.

REH

Let the word of Christ richly dwell within you,
with all wisdom teaching and admonishing one another
with psalms, hymns, and spiritual songs,
singing with thankfulness in your hearts to God.
Colossians 3:16

LONG RANGE:

Read your favorite Psalm aloud to each other.

5:00 AM	10:00 AM	2:00 PM	4:00 PM	5:00 PM
58	71	84	85	85

Let's go to church 9:30 or 11 a.m. upstairs.

I love you and want you with me at church.

I love you and want you with me everywhere.

I love you and want you with me all the time.

REH

For the grace of God has appeared, bringing salvation to all people,
instructing us to deny ungodliness and worldly desires and to live sensibly, righteously,
and in a godly manner in the present age, looking for the blessed hope
and the appearing of the glory of our great God and Savior, Christ Jesus,
who gave Himself for us to redeem us from every lawless deed,
and to purify for Himself a people for His own possession, eager for good deeds.
Titus 2:11-14

LONG RANGE:

How do you serve God?

5:00 AM	10:00 AM	2:00 PM	4:00 PM	5:00 PM
52	66	78	79	79

Faith over fear, that is R & E.

Our God is higher than everything.

Love rules for us.

I love you truly and will always.

REH

There is only one God, the Father, from whom are all things, and we exist for Him;

and one Lord, Jesus Christ, by whom are all things, and we exist through Him.

1 Corinthians 8:6

LONG RANGE:

What are your fears? How do you deal with them?

5:00 AM	10:00 AM	2:00 PM	4:00 PM	5:00 PM
59	70	75	77	73

May rain this afternoon.

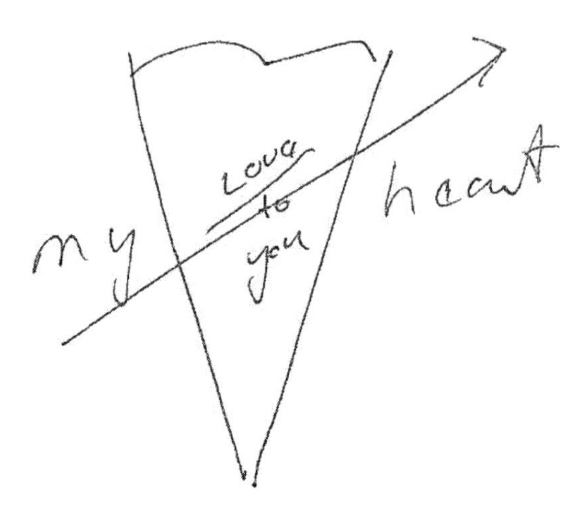

belongs to you!

I love you.

REH

Blessed are the pure in heart, for they will see God.

Matthew 5:8

LONG RANGE:

Draw a heart note for your spouse.

5:00 AM	10:00 AM	2:00 PM	4:00 PM	5:00 PM
73	82	93	93	93

Noon 90.

Love to you this Day of the Lord.

I always try to do what you suggest.

You never mean harm only good.

You are the Best of the Best.

I am so glad you are my wife.

I love you.

Forever.

REH

Listen to advice and accept discipline,

So that you may be wise the rest of your days.

Proverbs 19:20

LONG RANGE:

Do you seek advice from each other? Do you follow or ignore advice given?

5:00 AM	10:00 AM	2:00 PM	4:00 PM	5:00 PM
48	61	70	72	72

Cooler all day.

Remember what the doctor said. We just must be still and wait on the Lord!

God is so good to you and me.

Let us PRAISE His name.

I just love being with you – shelter-in-place or shelter-out-of-place.

REH

Wait for the Lord;

Be strong and let your heart take courage;

Yes, wait for the Lord.

Psalm 27:14

LONG RANGE:

When was the last time you waited for the Lord to answer a prayer or to move in your life? What did you do while you waited?

5:00 AM	10:00 AM	2:00 PM	4:00 PM	5:00 PM
50	63	72	72	72

May rain this afternoon.

I have love for you that you have not seen yet.

Why?

Because it is new, and it (love for you) grows each day.

I just love you and love just being with you.

U R MY LIFE.

REH

No one has ever seen God;

if we love one another, God remains in us,

and His love is perfected in us.

1 John 4:12

LONG RANGE:

Name something new in your relationship.

5:00 AM	10:00 AM	2:00 PM	4:00 PM	5:00 PM
57	63	73	75	75

Slow-down is not all that bad. I love the pace.

I love just being with you, doing whatever.

Trip (yes!) in near future.

I can see the ocean.

I love you more as each day passes.

REH

Oh, that I had wings like a dove!

I would fly away and be at rest.

Behold, I would flee far away,

I would spend my nights in the wilderness.

Psalm 55:6-7

LONG RANGE:

What is your life's pace right now? Is it time to slow down or speed up? Or is it just right?

5:00 AM	10:00 AM	2:00 PM	4:00 PM	5:00 PM
61	63	64	64	68

Cooler all day.

Just love here.

Of course – for you!

I love you!

REH

Make my joy complete by being of the same mind, maintaining the same love, united in spirit, intent on one purpose.

Philippians 2:2

LONG RANGE:

United in spirit – what does that mean to you?

5:00 AM	10:00 AM	2:00 PM	4:00 PM	5:00 PM
57	63	66	66	66

Cooler all day.

SORRY is all I have to say.

I stumble but God picks me up.

Sorry.

REH

Therefore, confess your sins to one another, and pray for one another

so that you may be healed.

A prayer of a righteous person, when it is brought about,

can accomplish much.

James 5:16

LONG RANGE:

Do you need to say you're sorry? Do you need to offer forgiveness?

5:00 AM	10:00 AM	2:00 PM	4:00 PM	5:00 PM
51	62	72	74	75

Warmer today.

Much better evening for both of us.

I just love you and really do just love being with you (it matters not where or what we R doing)

Just being with you is what matters.

Love you.

REH

But we urge you, brothers and sisters, to excel even more,

and to make it your ambition to lead a quiet life and attend to your own business

and work with your hands, just as we instructed you,

so that you will behave properly toward outsiders and not be in any need.

1 Thessalonians 4:11-12

LONG RANGE:

Do you have any special evening routines? What do you like most about them? Least?

5:00 AM	10:00 AM	2:00 PM	4:00 PM	5:00 PM
49	58	68	71	71

Cool all day. Sunshine!

Love = everything.

We have it.

We will always have it.

Love = everything.

God is LOVE.

I love you.

REH

I have been crucified with Christ; and it is no longer I who live, but Christ lives in me;

and the life which I now live in the flesh I live by faith in the Son of God,

who loved me and gave Himself up for me.

Galatians 2:20

LONG RANGE:

At the top of a page, write "Love =" then write seven lines about your spouse. Then, write seven more lines about God.

5:00 AM	10:00 AM	2:00 PM	4:00 PM	5:00 PM
70	72	73	75	75

Cloudy. Not as warm as yesterday.

Just love, nothing else here for you.

Love is all that is needed.

God is love.

We should love all.

I love you more and more.

REH

For the whole Law is fulfilled in one word, in the statement,

"You shall love your neighbor as yourself."

Galatians 5:14

LONG RANGE:

Think about your family and friends. How can you share some love with one of them as a couple this week?

5:00 AM	10:00 AM	2:00 PM	4:00 PM	5:00 PM
63	61	72	73	73

Cloudy – like yesterday.

REH loves EHH.

REH loves being with EHH,

No matter where, no matter what we are doing.

Just love all around us.

REH

Therefore, whether you eat or drink, or whatever you do, do all things for the glory of God.

1 Corinthians 10:31

LONG RANGE:

Prepare a meal together, for each other and for the glory of God.

5:00 AM	10:00 AM	2:00 PM	4:00 PM	5:00 PM
48	51	61	65	66

Cool like yesterday. Sunshine.

Already mid-week. Cannot believe it.

However, time with you is always good time, no matter how fast it goes.

Love Essie.

REH

If possible, so far as it depends on you, be at peace with all people.

Romans 12:18

LONG RANGE:

Take a short breather mid-week. Go for a walk, take a nap, call a friend, go fishing. Something to refresh and restore.

5:00 AM	10:00 AM	2:00 PM	4:00 PM	5:00 PM
61	63	68	66	66

Much cooler today.

Love just for you!

REH

Love is patient, love is kind, it is not jealous; love does not brag, it is not arrogant.
It does not act disgracefully, it does not seek its own benefit; it is not provoked,
does not keep an account of a wrong suffered, it does not rejoice in unrighteousness,
but rejoices with the truth; it keeps every confidence,
it believes all things, hopes all things, endures all things.

1 Corinthians 13:4-7

LONG RANGE:

Are you a patient person? How can you show more patience toward your spouse this week?

5:00 AM	10:00 AM	2:00 PM	4:00 PM	5:00 PM
65	66	75	78	78

May rain this morning, 40% chance.

You and I will be alright.

If God be for us who in the world can be (or succeed) against us.

I love you and just plain love being with you doing whatever.

I love you!

REH

No weapon formed against you shall prosper,

And every tongue which rises against you in judgment

You shall condemn.

This is the heritage of the servants of the Lord,

And their righteousness is from Me,"

Says the Lord.

Isaiah 54:17 (NKJ)

LONG RANGE:

Do you ever feel like the whole world is against you? God says no weapon formed against you shall prosper. Memorize that truth and repeat it to yourself as needed.

5:00 AM	10:00 AM	2:00 PM	4:00 PM	5:00 PM
55	59	68	70	72

Fog. Fog. May rain in afternoon.

Starting another week with the person I love most and love most being with.

That person is you.

I love you.

REH.

The reward of humility and the fear of the Lord

Are riches, honor, and life.

Proverbs 22:4

LONG RANGE:

What are some of your spouse's traits that you admire most?

5:00 AM	10:00 AM	2:00 PM	4:00 PM	5:00 PM
63	66	82	84	86

Summer temps.

Love that is overflowing for you and you only.

I love you!

REH

Jesus said,

"Whoever believes in me, as the Scripture has said,

'Out of his heart will flow rivers of living water.'"

John 7:38 (ESV)

LONG RANGE:

What does "living water" mean to you?

5:00 AM	10:00 AM	2:00 PM	4:00 PM	5:00 PM
68	69	81	85	86

Like summer.

LOVE LOVE LOVE

That is all I can think of about you this morning.

Love you.

REH

In the morning, Lord, You will hear my voice;

In the morning I will present my prayer to You and be on the watch.

Psalm 5:3

LONG RANGE:

Do you have a morning routine? How does it affect the rest of your day?

5:00 AM	10:00 AM	2:00 PM	4:00 PM	5:00 PM
57	63	75	81	81

Sunbathing – yea.

Life is but a vapor.

Therefore, we should live it like God desires for us.

Our life together is God's plan for us and we are living it for God's glory.

I just love you so much.

We will get through this.

REH

He will fulfill the desire of those who fear Him;

He will also hear their cry for help and save them.

Psalm 145:19

LONG RANGE:

Have you ever thought about God's plan for you as a couple? What do you think that plan might be?

5:00 AM	10:00 AM	2:00 PM	4:00 PM	5:00 PM
66	70	79	81	81

Rain this morning, sun this afternoon.

I love you.

That is it and that is the way it will always be.

REH

Jesus said,

"God is spirit, and those who worship Him must worship in spirit and truth."

John 4:24

LONG RANGE:

Which season is your favorite? What do you like most about it?

5:00 AM	10:00 AM	2:00 PM	4:00 PM	5:00 PM
68	84	94	94	94

REH loves EHH.

That is a fact!

That will always be.

LOVE YOU.

REH

We can breakfast together after court @ 8 or 8:15.

REH

Behold, I stand at the door and knock; if anyone hears My voice and opens the door,

I will come in to him and will dine with him, and he with Me.

Revelation 3:20

LONG RANGE:

How often do you share breakfast together? What are your favorite breakfast foods?

5:00 AM	10:00 AM	2:00 PM	4:00 PM	5:00 PM
71	83	94	95	95

Another week started.

Start it with LOVE.

Love for God, you, and others.

Love rules over all.

I love you. <

I love you. <

REH

Jesus said,

"I am giving you a new commandment, that you love one another;

just as I have loved you, that you also love one another."

John 13:34

LONG RANGE:

Do something tangible to express your love to one another this week.

5:00 AM	10:00 AM	2:00 PM	4:00 PM	5:00 PM
61	70	80	80	79

Love will see us through all things.

God is our strength.

You are my life.

REH

The Lord of armies is with us;

The God of Jacob is our stronghold.

Psalm 46:11

LONG RANGE:

When have you felt God's strength the most?

5:00 AM	10:00 AM	2:00 PM	4:00 PM	5:00 PM
62	72	83	84	84

Sill very warm.

Good job yesterday.

I just love being wherever you are.

Ok? Ok.

Love you.

REH

Commit your work to the Lord,

and your plans will be established.

Proverbs 16:3

LONG RANGE:

Pray together and commit your work to the Lord this week.

MOTHER'S
DAY

5:00 AM	10:00 AM	2:00 PM	4:00 PM	5:00 PM
68	82	91	93	93

Love over and over for you this morning.

Start the week off with LOVE.

REH

Loves EHH

Let your fountain be blessed,

and rejoice in the wife of your youth,

a lovely deer, a graceful doe.

Proverbs 5:18-19

LONG RANGE:

Name something about your spouse brings you joy?

5:00 AM	10:00 AM	2:00 PM	4:00 PM	5:00 PM
65	81	90	92	92

Just to be where you are. That is all I want.

I love you and love being with you.

REH

Jesus said,

"But seek first the kingdom of God and His righteousness,

and all these things will be added to you."

Matthew 6:33

LONG RANGE:

What do you want most out of your marriage?

5:00 AM	10:00 AM	2:00 PM	4:00 PM	5:00 PM
63	66	73	75	75

Nice, top-down weather.

Another week just flies by.

All of them are very good as long as you fly by with me.

REH who

Loves EHH

Every good thing given and every perfect gift is from above,

coming down from the Father of lights,

with whom there is no variation or shifting shadow.

James 1:17

LONG RANGE:

Take some pictures together this week and print them out to display in your home.

5:00 AM	10:00 AM	2:00 PM	4:00 PM	5:00 PM
60	62	75	77	77

Love for you just keeps on growing.

I cannot control it.

It is out of control for you.

REH

I love Essie.

REH

I can do all things through Christ who strengthens me.

Philippians 4:13 (NKJV)

LONG RANGE:

What's the hardest thing you've ever had to do? Did you experience God's strength through it?

5:00 AM	10:00 AM	2:00 PM	4:00 PM	5:00 PM
66	71	82	85	86

REH loves EHH.

EHH makes REH complete

in God's eyes. Amen.

REH w/ love

For the eyes of the Lord are on the righteous,

And His ears are open to their prayers.

1 Peter 3:12

LONG RANGE:

How does your spouse "complete" you?

5:00 AM	10:00 AM	2:00 PM	4:00 PM	5:00 PM
48	61	73	75	77

Warmer today. 1 p.m. 72 and sunshine.

Today is the day we honor you as the "Best Mom in the World."

You deserve all honors.

You are very special and you make those around you feel special.

You are God's servant here on earth.

Keep it up.

PTL for you.

I love you.

REH

Behold, children are a gift of the Lord,

The fruit of the womb is a reward.

Psalm 127:3

LONG RANGE:

What did you love most about your own mother when you were a child? If you are a mom now, what do you love most about being a mom?

5:00 AM	10:00 AM	2:00 PM	4:00 PM	5:00 PM
66	72	83	85	86

Let love rule your life.

Let peace be with you.

Let ME be your BFF and I will always take care of you (as long as able).

You may wind up taking care of me.

Love,

REH

Jesus said,

"These things I have spoken to you, that in Me you may have peace.

In the world you will have tribulation; but be of good cheer,

I have overcome the world."

John 16:33

LONG RANGE:

Is your home a place of peace? How could it be more peaceful? Spend some time praying together as you walk through your home.

5:00 AM	10:00 AM	2:00 PM	4:00 PM	5:00 PM
60	60	65	66	65

Not as warm as yesterday.

You have a function tonight. Do not forget.

I will take care of that for you.

I am your helper and partner-in-life.

We do all things together for God's glory.

I love you.

REH

Worthy are You, our Lord and our God, to receive glory and honor and power;
for You created all things, and because of Your will
they existed, and were created.
Revelation 4:11

LONG RANGE:

How does your spouse help you most?

5:00 AM	10:00 AM	2:00 PM	4:00 PM	5:00 PM
46	52	68	70	70

Real nice this afternoon. Enjoy!

I love you now and always will.

Nothing can change that.

Love,

REH

Let's not love with word or with tongue, but in deed and truth.

1 John 3:18

LONG RANGE:

How do each of you cope with change in your lives?

5:00 AM	10:00 AM	2:00 PM	4:00 PM	5:00 PM
57	63	73	75	75

Real nice today.

I just love you.

It is simple as that, and that is the way it will always be.

Love to you from

REH

Jesus said,

"Heaven and earth will pass away, but My words will not pass away."

Matthew 24:35

LONG RANGE:

What role does respect play in your relationship?

5:00 AM	10:00 AM	2:00 PM	4:00 PM	5:00 PM
47	50	57	59	59

Cool all day.

I liked last night.

Let us do it more.

Do you know what I mean?

Ok ok.

Love you!

REH

Marriage is to be held in honor among all.

Hebrews 13:4

LONG RANGE:

What does intimacy mean in your marriage? Read this article together to enhance your conversation. "Marital Intimacy is More than Sex," by Josh Squires, https://www.desiringgod.org/articles/marital-intimacy-is-more-than-sex.

5:00 AM	10:00 AM	2:00 PM	4:00 PM	5:00 PM
61	63	73	73	73

The beach should be warmer.

Let's go. I am ready.

I love just being with you either here or the beach or anywhere.

Love you.

REH

And He said, "My presence shall go with you, and I will give you rest."

Exodus 33:14

LONG RANGE:

Get outside and enjoy each other's company.

5:00 AM	10:00 AM	2:00 PM	4:00 PM	5:00 PM
64	**66**	**73**	**73**	**73**

I may have had a bad day, but I serve a good God.

Slow down, Bobby Boy, and get things right like you use to.

Ok. Ok. I hear me.

I love you so much and more each day we are together.

Love you.

REH

Do not be conformed to this world, but be transformed
by the renewal of your mind,
that by testing you may discern what is the will of God,
what is good and acceptable and perfect.
Romans 12:2 (ESV)

LONG RANGE:

When was your last bad day? Did your spouse help you get through it?

"God knows
the rhythm of my spirit
And knows my heart's thoughts.
He is as close as breathing."
~ Estelle H. Herndon

5:00 AM	10:00 AM	2:00 PM	4:00 PM	5:00 PM
61	65	69	68	68

Cool all day.

I am at my best when you are by my side.

Always remember that!

I love you.

I love being with you.

REH

Do your best to present yourself to God as one approved,

a worker who has no need to be ashamed,

rightly handling the word of truth.

2 Timothy 2:15 (ESV)

LONG RANGE:

When was the last time you felt at your best? What helped you feel that way?

5:00 AM	10:00 AM	2:00 PM	4:00 PM	5:00 PM
69	69	73	74	74

Rain.

Hope your energy is restored.

Love to see you running and doing.

Love to see you anyway.

Just love being with you.

REH

For this purpose I also labor,

striving according to His power which works mightily within me.

Colossians 1:29

LONG RANGE:

What have you done recently that is considered self-care? Do your self-care efforts affect your energy levels?

5:00 AM	10:00 AM	2:00 PM	4:00 PM	5:00 PM
73	74	76	67	65

Rain probably today; cool this evening with 40% chance of rain.

Today, our last day on the beach.

I thank God for being able to serve.

God is with God.

We cannot fail.

If God is for us, who can be against us.

You and me serving God.

Love you.

REH

You shall follow the Lord your God and fear Him;

and you shall keep His commandments, listen to His voice,

serve Him, and cling to Him.

Deuteronomy 13:4

LONG RANGE:

What does it mean to you to fear God?

5:00 AM	10:00 AM	2:00 PM	4:00 PM	5:00 PM
63	66	78	81	81

Time passes so fast.

Another week to start.

But it is all okay as long as you are by my side.

You are what keeps me going.

You are my all.

REH

Blessed is the man who remains steadfast under trial,

for when he has stood the test he will receive the crown of life,

which God has promised to those who love him.

James 1:12 (ESV)

LONG RANGE:

Think of a recent trial you both recently faced. Were you able to remain steadfast?

5:00 AM	10:00 AM	2:00 PM	4:00 PM	5:00 PM
67	67	68	68	67

Cool all day. Rain.

Rainy and cool today.

Dress for your warmth.

Love that is just for you from me.

Ok. Ok.

Love you.

REH

Then he prayed again, and heaven gave rain, and the earth bore its fruit.

James 5:18 (ESV)

LONG RANGE:

Find a classic, romantic movie to watch together during your free time. (Great suggestions on IMDB: https://www.imdb.com/list/ls033232397/)

5:00 AM	10:00 AM	2:00 PM	4:00 PM	5:00 PM
69	66	75	77	76

So glad you are better.

Your eyes are doing well.

PTL PTL for everything.

My love for you grows each day.

You and me forever and ever.

Our God is awesome.

REH

Love you

Open my eyes, that I may behold

wondrous things out of your law.

Psalm 119:18 (ESV)

LONG RANGE:

Spend 30 seconds looking each other in the eyes, noticing colors, shapes, sizes, and the love flowing from them. Then write your spouse a love note about your experience.

I love you, Robert Herndon,

with all my

forever.

Thank you.

Essie

5:00 AM	10:00 AM	2:00 PM	4:00 PM	5:00 PM
52	59	75	79	78

Another week starting.

Another week with the one I love the most.

Another week together, just REH/EHH as it should be.

Rejoice. This is God's day.

Love just to you.

REH

Must start on major clean-up on house.

I will greatly rejoice in the Lord;

my soul shall exult in my God,

for he has clothed me with the garments of salvation;

he has covered me with the robe of righteousness,

as a bridegroom decks himself like a priest with a beautiful headdress,

and as a bride adorns herself with her jewels.

Isaiah 61:10 (ESV)

LONG RANGE:

What's the last major project you tackled together? How did it go? Is it time to plan another one?

5:00 AM	10:00 AM	2:00 PM	4:00 PM	5:00 PM
59	58	61	62	62

Cool all day. Rain, too.

Love abounds for you!

Do you know that?

You are my wife.

You are my life.

You are my all.

Do not ever forget or take that lightly.

I mean it.

REH

Jesus said to him,

"I am the way, and the truth, and the life. No one comes to the Father except through me.

John 14:6 (ESV)

LONG RANGE:

Did you recite marriage vows at your wedding? Do you remember them? Try to recall some of them, and discuss what they mean to you now.

5:00 AM	10:00 AM	2:00 PM	4:00 PM	5:00 PM
57	62	76	78	78

Warmer than yesterday.

Sunday – our day for our Lord.

Let us go and worship together.

Together always, you and me.

REH

Love Essie

REH

And let us consider how to stir up one another to love and good works,

not neglecting to meet together, as is the habit of some,

but encouraging one another, and all the more as you see the Day drawing near.

Hebrews 10:24-25 (ESV)

LONG RANGE:

Do you have couple friends? Friends that you get together with as a couple to have fun, relax, fellowship together? If not, do you find this missing in your life or not? If so, make a plan to meet new friends. If you have friends like this already, plan a date with them.

5:00 AM	10:00 AM	2:00 PM	4:00 PM	5:00 PM
64	66	73	76	75

May rain.

The day of recovery is at hand.

You will be much better today PTL.

I love you and want to take care of you.

I love you. That is it.

REH

The Lord sustains him on his sickbed;

in his illness you restore him to full health.

Psalm 41:3 (ESV)

LONG RANGE:

To continue the discussion on wedding vows, were part of yours, "in sickness and in health"? Do you see this vow differently now than you did on your wedding day?

5:00 AM	10:00 AM	2:00 PM	4:00 PM	5:00 PM
68	70	78	79	79

Just love this morning.

So glad you are doing better.

PTL.

REH

Let them praise your great and awesome name!

Holy is he!

Psalm 99:3 (ESV)

LONG RANGE:

Pray together, praising God and thanking Him for His goodness.

5:00 AM	10:00 AM	2:00 PM	4:00 PM	5:00 PM
75	85	94	93	92

Yesterday much better from the day before, don't you agree?

Nothing here for you this morning but

LOVE LOVE LOVE LOVE LOVE and more LOVE.

REH

Let your steadfast love, O Lord, be upon us,

even as we hope in you.

Psalm 33:22 (ESV)

LONG RANGE:

Doodle some artwork for your spouse, incorporating his/her name, hearts, and the word LOVE.

5:00 AM	10:00 AM	2:00 PM	4:00 PM	5:00 PM
76	83	91	91	92

Love that grows each day for you, more and more.

Do not forget that.

REH

Many waters cannot quench love,

neither can floods drown it.

Song of Solomon 8:7 (ESV)

LONG RANGE:

Depending on your space, plant flowers, vegetables, herbs, or even a tree together this week.

5:00 AM	10:00 AM	2:00 PM	4:00 PM	5:00 PM
74	84	93	94	93

Love and more love for you

This bright morning.

REH + EHH

Always

Satisfy us in the morning with your steadfast love,

that we may rejoice and be glad all our days.

Psalm 90:14 (ESV)

LONG RANGE:

Plan to wake early one morning, just to do something fun together.

5:00 AM	10:00 AM	2:00 PM	4:00 PM	5:00 PM
74	86	95	95	95

Real hot today.

Love you so much.

You are my Dream Girl.

You are my all.

I love you.

REH

Behold, you are beautiful, my love,

behold, you are beautiful!

Song of Solomon 4:1 (ESV)

LONG RANGE:

Compliment your spouse.

5:00 AM	10:00 AM	2:00 PM	4:00 PM	5:00 PM
58	63	72	76	75

Nice. You will like it.

I love you SOOOOOOOO much.

Ok?

U make me COMPLETE.

REH

Jesus said,

"Give to everyone who begs from you,

and from one who takes away your goods do not demand them back.

And as you wish that others would do to you, do so to them."

Luke 6:30-31 (ESV)

LONG RANGE:

How does the Golden Rule apply in your marriage? (The last line in the verse above.)

5:00 AM	10:00 AM	2:00 PM	4:00 PM	5:00 PM
64	67	79	82	82

Beach here we are!

Today let us go unto the Lord's house.

Let us sing and praise our Lord.

Let us show our LOVE for the Lord and each other to all who see us.

REH

Love EHH.

O Lord, I love the habitation of your house

and the place where your glory dwells.

Psalm 26:8 (ESV)

LONG RANGE:

Sing an old hymn or a new contemporary worship song together, softly, worshiping the Lord together in song.

5:00 AM	10:00 AM	2:00 PM	4:00 PM	5:00 PM
62	74	88	90	90

Another week.

Another week of more love for you.

REH loves EHH.

REH

Before the mountains were brought forth,

Or ever You had formed the earth and the world,

Even from everlasting to everlasting, You are God.

Psalm 90:2 (NKJV)

LONG RANGE:

What do you like most about mountains? Do you have favorite mountains?

5:00 AM	10:00 AM	2:00 PM	4:00 PM	5:00 PM
69	80	91	93	92

Hot.

You were a super greeter last night.

The event went well. I enjoyed helping.

Love just for you.

REH

I love you!

Greet one another with a kiss of love.

Peace to you all who are in Christ Jesus. Amen.

1 Peter 5:14 (NKJV)

LONG RANGE:

Praise your spouse for a recent job well done.

5:00 AM	10:00 AM	2:00 PM	4:00 PM	5:00 PM
70	80	91	93	93

Rather warm.

I love the way you help me and take care of me.

I just love being with you.

REH

Love you!!

Bear one another's burdens, and so fulfill the law of Christ.

Galatians 6:2 (NKJV)

LONG RANGE:

Ask your spouse what you can do better to take care of them. Listen and actually hear his/her answer.

5:00 AM	10:00 AM	2:00 PM	4:00 PM	5:00 PM
71	81	92	94	94

Only LOVE is here for you.

LOVE ONLY

And just for you.

REH

Jesus said,

"Give, and it will be given to you.

Good measure, pressed down, shaken together, running over,

will be put into your lap.

For with the measure you use it will be measured back to you."

Luke 6:38 (ESV)

LONG RANGE:

Make a plan to give something to a stranger in need.

5:00 AM	10:00 AM	2:00 PM	4:00 PM	5:00 PM
73	82	94	95	95

More love just for you!

And it shall be FOREVER.

Love,

REH

And there is salvation in no one else,
for there is no other name under heaven
given among men by which we must be saved.
Acts 4:12 (NKJV)

LONG RANGE:

Are you saved? What does your salvation mean to you?

5:00 AM	10:00 AM	2:00 PM	4:00 PM	5:00 PM
70	83	95	96	96

Tomorrow is BIG DAY!

My prayer is that you have many more tomorrows.

I love you and always will.

You are my dream girl.

REH

LOVE

Jesus said,

"Therefore I tell you, whatever you ask in prayer,

believe that you have received it,

and it will be yours."

Mark 11:24

LONG RANGE:

Are you a dreamer? Do you dream together, or is one of you the dreamer and the other not so much? What are some of your dreams you've never shared before?

5:00 AM	10:00 AM	2:00 PM	4:00 PM	5:00 PM
68	79	88	91	91

Nothing here but LOVE.

However, there is a lot of LOVE here and it is all for you.

REH

God shows his love for us in that while we were still sinners, Christ died for us.

Romans 5:8 (ESV)

LONG RANGE:

What does your spouse do or say that makes you feel the most loved?

5:00 AM	10:00 AM	2:00 PM	4:00 PM	5:00 PM
73	81	89	88	85

Just 1 ½ days left.

I am READY to go now!

Love you so and just love being with you.

REH

Therefore you also must be ready,

for the Son of Man is coming

at an hour you do not expect.

Matthew 24:44 (ESV)

LONG RANGE:

Do you prepare for the future? Discuss how you can help each other prepare for different aspects of your future.

6 am 54

10 am 61

2 pm 70

4 pm 70

5 pm 70

cloudy

Cool today

Well, another week finished.
We had a good work-week
and accomplished much.
As I said before, you quit,
I quit, I cannot do w/o
you. I Love you and Love
you being by my side ALL THE
time.
PTL our GOD who continues
show his favor upon us.

[signature]

5:00 AM	10:00 AM	2:00 PM	4:00 PM	5:00 PM
70	79	93	95	94

Always remember you and I will be all right.

If God is for us, who can be against us.

Amen Amen Amen

Love just for you.

I will have your breakfast at the office for T to see.

REH

Why? Because I love you.

Love to Essie.

REH

Jesus said to them, "Come and have breakfast."

Now none of the disciples dared ask him, "Who are you?"

They knew it was the Lord.

John 21:12 (ESV)

LONG RANGE:

Discuss different ways you can stand up for each other when faced with negativity from family or friends.

5:00 AM	10:00 AM	2:00 PM	4:00 PM	5:00 PM
67	70	76	76	75

Another day to tell you I love you more than anything.

You make me COMPLETE.

I love you.

REH

Jesus said,

"As the Father has loved me, so have I loved you. Abide in my love."

John 15:9 (ESV)

LONG RANGE:

Choose two days in the coming weeks. One day for each of you focus on the other – go somewhere the other wants to go or do something the other wants to do – but do it together. (A few examples might include shopping, fishing, bowling, hiking, flea markets, spa, or sporting events. The list is endless but should fit your budget and circumstances without causing stress.)

5:00 AM	10:00 AM	2:00 PM	4:00 PM	5:00 PM
74	81	91	92	91

Warmer today.

Another week almost gone by.

However, as the weeks go by my love for you GROWS AND GROWS.

Remember that.

REH

Love EHH.

Grow in the grace and knowledge of our Lord and Savior Jesus Christ.

To him be the glory both now and to the day of eternity.

2 Peter 3:18 (ESV)

LONG RANGE:

In what ways would you like to grow in the coming year? Discuss how to make that happen.

5:00 AM	10:00 AM	2:00 PM	4:00 PM	5:00 PM
72	82	89	87	86

You have been prayed over.

REH LOVES EHH.

Always love for you.

Forever together.

Love, REH

Oh, magnify the Lord with me,

and let us exalt his name together!

Psalm 34:3 (ESV)

LONG RANGE:

Take turns praying over each other.

5:00 AM	10:00 AM	2:00 PM	4:00 PM	5:00 PM
73	79	84	84	84

So glad you and I are better.

I was fearful for you yesterday.

I am good this morning.

I love you.

NOW and ALWAYS.

REH

For God has not given us a spirit of fear, but of power and of love and of a sound mind.

2 Timothy 1:7 (NKJV)

LONG RANGE:

Growing up, did you have any fears? How did you overcome them?

5:00 AM	10:00 AM	2:00 PM	4:00 PM	5:00 PM
60	72	81	83	83

Another week ending.

Another week with love for you that never ends.

Love you now and forever,

Love you more and more as

I am around you.

Love REH

For by one offering He has perfected forever those who are being sanctified.

Hebrews 10:14 (NKJV)

LONG RANGE:

What does sanctified mean to you personally?

5:00 AM	10:00 AM	2:00 PM	4:00 PM	5:00 PM
65	74	83	84	83

You are so special, to me and many others.

You are my Dream Girl.

You are my everything.

Love, REH

Love you!!

But the very hairs of your head are all numbered.

Do not fear therefore; you are of more value than many sparrows.

Matthew 10:30-31 (NKJV)

LONG RANGE:

Take turns filling in this blank about your spouse: "You are of more value than ____________."
Have fun expressing your love this way.

5:00 AM	10:00 AM	2:00 PM	4:00 PM	5:00 PM
75	84	91	90	90

The year is half over.

Time moves on quickly.

As long as it is with you, I am OKAY.

I love you.

I love being with you.

REH

But do not let this one fact escape your notice, beloved,

that with the Lord one day is like a thousand years,

and a thousand years like one day.

2 Peter 3:8

LONG RANGE:

Does the second half of the year speed by for you? Be intentional with your planning this year and incorporate special times just for the two of you.

5:00 AM	10:00 AM	2:00 PM	4:00 PM	5:00 PM
73	84	91	93	93

Hot!

Another week starting.

It is all okay with me as long as you are with me.

Wherever, whatever, just you with me, that's what counts with me.

I love you!

REH

Jesus Christ is the same yesterday and today, and forever.

Hebrews 13:8

LONG RANGE:

Change is such a part of our lives. How does the thought that Jesus is the same yesterday, today, and forever resonate with you and your faith?

5:00 AM	10:00 AM	2:00 PM	4:00 PM	5:00 PM
70	75	82	82	82

Rain 50% chance.

Nothing but love here.

That is love for you.

That is all that is here.

LOVE LOVE LOVE

All for YOU YOU YOU.

I love you!

REH

Let love be genuine.

Abhor what is evil; hold fast to what is good.

Romans 12:9

(ESV)

LONG RANGE:

What's your favorite flower? Draw any flower for your spouse.

5:00 AM	10:00 AM	2:00 PM	4:00 PM	5:00 PM
68	81	90	90	86

May rain in the afternoon.

Father's Day was wonderful for this father.

Great being with you and the children.

You are my BFF and you will always be my BFF.

We are ONE and our job is to honor God who made us ONE.

I love you, BFF.

REH

"Therefore a man shall leave his father and mother and hold fast to his wife,

and the two shall become one flesh."

Ephesians 5:31

(ESV)

LONG RANGE:

Share some favorite memories about time spent with your dads. If you are a dad, what's your favorite part of being a dad?

5:00 AM	10:00 AM	2:00 PM	4:00 PM	5:00 PM
57	60	59	58	58

Rain.

Rain again, Love again.

Love for you is there every morning you get up – rain or shine.

Do not forget that.

Start your day by being loved.

REH, who loves you

"I will make showers fall in their season; they will be showers of blessing."

Ezekiel 34:26

LONG RANGE:

If you don't already have a Scripture memory plan in place, start today. Memorize together one Scripture verse a week, helping, challenging, and encouraging each other as you go through the week. Today's is a short one that could get you started.

5:00 AM	10:00 AM	2:00 PM	4:00 PM	5:00 PM
71	76	84	84	83

Glad you got shoe insert.

Maybe we are on the road to better feet.

Love just being with you.

You are my SUNSHINE.

Love,

REH

Your word is a lamp to my feet

And a light to my path.

Psalm 119:105 (NKJV)

LONG RANGE:

Wash and/or massage each other's feet.

5:00 AM	10:00 AM	2:00 PM	4:00 PM	5:00 PM
74	80	88	89	88

Holidays are nice, but they are much better when I am with you,

as this 4th.

Love to you.

REH

Blessed is the nation whose God is the Lord,

The people He has chosen as His own inheritance.

Psalm 33:12 (NKJV)

LONG RANGE:

Watch some fireworks together.

5:00 AM	10:00 AM	2:00 PM	4:00 PM	5:00 PM
72	71	72	73	73

Cool all day. Beautiful weather.

We shall overcome!

We (not just me) are on OVERLOAD.

This too will pass.

All will be OK as God works out things for our good.

Amen.

Love you.

REH

Therefore we do not lose heart.

Even though our outward man is perishing, yet the inward man is being renewed day by day.

For our light affliction, which is but for a moment,

is working for us a far more exceeding and eternal weight of glory,

while we do not look at the things which are seen, but at the things which are not seen.

For the things which are seen are temporary, but the things which are not seen are eternal.

2 Corinthians 4:16-18

LONG RANGE:

Is your schedule on overload right now? Pray for each other, asking for strength and wisdom. Then discuss ways you can help lighten each other's load.

5:00 AM	10:00 AM	2:00 PM	4:00 PM	5:00 PM
77	86	94	93	93

Only love for my only woman

And it is forever and ever.

Love Essie.

REH

And it shall come to pass

That whoever calls on the name of the Lord

Shall be saved.

Acts 2:21 (NKJV)

LONG RANGE:

Find a love poem and recite it to your spouse.

5:00 AM	10:00 AM	2:00 PM	4:00 PM	5:00 PM
72	82	90	90	91

Love that is for you only.

Love that will always be for you only.

Ok?

REH

"I am the Alpha and the Omega, the Beginning and the End,"

says the Lord,

"who is and who was and who is to come, the Almighty."

Revelation 1:8 (NKJV)

LONG RANGE:

How did your romance begin? Do you still consider yourselves to be romantic?

5:00 AM	10:00 AM	2:00 PM	4:00 PM	5:00 PM
70	81	91	91	91

No coffee, Bobby Boy.

Getting ready for procedure.

I love you.

I love you being with me all the time and everywhere.

REH

Jesus said,

"Let not your hearts be troubled. Believe in God; believe also in me.

John 14:1 (ESV)

LONG RANGE:

Draw, paint, or doodle a sketch together.

5:00 AM	10:00 AM	2:00 PM	4:00 PM	5:00 PM
73	83	93	94	94

Never tire of writing notes to you.

Why?

'Cause I love you so.

You make my life complete.

You are my BFF and will always be my BFF.

REH loves EHH.

REH

As in water face reflects face,

So a man's heart reveals the man.

Proverbs 27:19 (NKJV)

LONG RANGE:

Write a love note to your spouse about being your friend.

5:00 AM	10:00 AM	2:00 PM	4:00 PM	5:00 PM
76	85	92	93	93

Hot.

Had a wonderful rest day with a wonderful woman.

Love you.

REH

Be still, and know that I am God;

I will be exalted among the nations,

I will be exalted in the earth!

Psalm 46:10 (NKJV)

LONG RANGE:

What's your favorite way to rest? Try to make it happen this week.

5:00 AM	10:00 AM	2:00 PM	4:00 PM	5:00 PM
75	81	88	88	88

Already Wednesday.

Time flies.

Time is much better with you in my presence.

Love for you.

REH, your BFF

Create in me a clean heart, O God,

And renew a steadfast spirit within me.

Do not cast me away from Your presence,

And do not take Your Holy Spirit from me.

Psalm 51:10-11 (NKJV)

LONG RANGE:

Create a story together about a fast-moving clock.

5:00 AM	10:00 AM	2:00 PM	4:00 PM	5:00 PM
77	82	89	90	89

Love that is just for you.

You make me better.

Love to YOU.

REH

Seek the Lord and His strength;

Seek His face evermore!

1 Chronicles 16:11 (NKJV)

LONG RANGE:

In what ways would you like to be a better you? How can your spouse help you achieve that?

5:00 AM	**10:00 AM**	**2:00 PM**	**4:00 PM**	**5:00 PM**
71	**78**	**88**	**88**	**88**

Believe me, our times are in God's hands.

It is what God says, not what we say.

Trust me because I am trusting God.

Love you.

REH

But now, O Lord,
You are our Father;
We are the clay, and You our potter;
And all we are the work of Your hand.
Isaiah 64:8 (NKJV)

LONG RANGE:

Hold hands for a few moments. Then examine each other's hands, lovingly caressing as you do.

5:00 AM	10:00 AM	2:00 PM	4:00 PM	5:00 PM
54	64	73	76	76

It is not just another day.

It is a day with the person I am in love with.

OK OK OK.

REH

LOVE YOU!

One person values one day over another, another values every day the same.

Each person must be fully convinced in his own mind.

Romans 14:5

LONG RANGE:

When was the last time you took your time kissing each other? Would now be a good time?

5:00 AM	10:00 AM	2:00 PM	4:00 PM	5:00 PM
52	65	76	78	79

Love to you from me.

You and me together forever.

REH

Oh, how great is Your goodness,

Which You have laid up for those who fear You,

Which You have prepared for those who trust in You

In the presence of the sons of men!

Psalm 31:19 (NKJV)

LONG RANGE:

Recall God's greatness in your life in as many ways as you can name, then give Him the thanks and glory for it all.

5:00 AM	10:00 AM	2:00 PM	4:00 PM	5:00 PM
70	79	87	87	86

To the house of the Lord we shall go.

Our God has blessed our marriage and blessed our lives sooo much.

Love,

REH, your BFF

One thing I have desired of the Lord,

That will I seek:

That I may dwell in the house of the Lord

All the days of my life,

To behold the beauty of the Lord,

And to inquire in His temple.

Psalm 27:4 (NKJV)

LONG RANGE:

Has God ever presented opportunities for you to be role models in your marriage to other couples? How did He use you? If this hasn't happened yet, are you open to serving Him in this way?

5:00 AM	10:00 AM	2:00 PM	4:00 PM	5:00 PM
68	81	94	97	96

Really hot.

If you are available, I would like to go on ANOTHER DATE with you.

Check

❑ Yes

Or

❑ No

REH

Nothing is better for a man than that he should eat and drink,

and that his soul should enjoy good in his labor.

This also, I saw, was from the hand of God.

Ecclesiastes 2:24 (NKJV)

LONG RANGE:

Write out a date invitation of your own and present it to your spouse. (Hint: if both of you do it, that means TWO dates!)

5:00 AM	10:00 AM	2:00 PM	4:00 PM	5:00 PM
71	82	97	97	97

Almost 100!

Today we start on our journey of helping others to understanding the power of the Spirit of God.

The Spirit is with us and will assist us all the way.

We want all to grow in the Spirit of God.

Love you!

REH

Do not quench the Spirit.

1 Thessalonians 5:19 (NKJV)

LONG RANGE:

What journey are you on for the Lord right now? Pray and ask the Holy Spirit to assist you along the way.

5:00 AM	10:00 AM	2:00 PM	4:00 PM	5:00 PM
75	79	91	93	91

REH Loves EHH.

I will absolutely try hard not to do what I did yesterday.

The whole day was a smear – all because of how I hurt you.

Love and forgive.

Love and forgive.

That is our policy.

REH

Be kind to one another, tenderhearted,

forgiving one another,

even as God in Christ forgave you.

Ephesians 4:32 (NKJV)

LONG RANGE:

Have you hurt your spouse recently?* Confess and ask, sincerely, for forgiveness. Talk through the hurt with love, compassion, kindness, understanding, and respect. (*See Notes at end of book.)

5:00 AM	10:00 AM	2:00 PM	4:00 PM	5:00 PM
76	84	93	92	91

Nothing here but LOVE for you.

REH loves EHH

And will FOREVER!

REH

Jesus said,

"I am the living bread which came down from heaven.

If anyone eats of this bread, he will live forever;

and the bread that I shall give is My flesh,

which I shall give for the life of the world."

John 6:51 (NKJV)

LONG RANGE:

When was the last time you took Communion together? Have you ever served Communion in your own home?

5:00 AM	10:00 AM	2:00 PM	4:00 PM	5:00 PM
74	84	94	95	94

I am so sorry.

I sinned against you.

I sinned against God.

We are not consumed because of God's mercies.

They are new every morning (right now).

Great is our God's faithfulness.

I shall do better because the Holy Spirit is with me and teaching me.

Love me as I love you.

You R My All.

REH

Through the Lord's mercies we are not consumed,

Because His compassions fail not.

They are new every morning;

Great is Your faithfulness.

Lamentations 3:22-23 (NKJV)

LONG RANGE:

Those hurts from the other day? Are you still holding onto them?* Time to let them go – God's mercies are new every morning. Start the day fresh – washed clean, forgiven. (* See note at the end of the book.)

5:00 AM	10:00 AM	2:00 PM	4:00 PM	5:00 PM
74	85	91	90	90

You did great last night.

We (REH/EHH) make a good team and are meant to be a TEAM.

Now and Forever.

Love you so much.

REH

For we are God's fellow workers; you are God's field, you are God's building.

1 Corinthians 3:9 (NKJV)

LONG RANGE:

How do you and your spouse make a good team?

5:00 AM	10:00 AM	2:00 PM	4:00 PM	5:00 PM
72	**78**	**88**	**88**	**85**

Oh how LOVE rules.

Love you so much and it rules my life.

Oh! Just being with you is my desire.

REH

And you will seek Me and find Me, when you search for Me with all your heart.

Jeremiah 29:13 (NKJV)

LONG RANGE:

Share one of your personal heart's desires with each other.

5:00 AM	10:00 AM	2:00 PM	4:00 PM	5:00 PM
72	78	91	93	92

Tag is coming.

The event will be completely over.

We must plan for our future as to a slow down; as to travel;

As to more LOVE, if that is possible.

Love you!

REH

There are many plans in a man's heart,

Nevertheless the Lord's counsel—that will stand.

Proverbs 19:21 (NKJV)

LONG RANGE:

Do you have any travel plans?

5:00 AM	10:00 AM	2:00 PM	4:00 PM	5:00 PM
68	81	94	96	95

Nothing here for you but LOVE and there is plenty of it for you.

I love you.

Our trip is at hand.

PTL PTL PTL.

Love you,

REH

By faith we understand that the universe was created by the word of God,

so that what is seen was not made out of things that are visible.

Hebrews 11:3 (ESV)

LONG RANGE:

Plan a road trip (real or pretend). Where will you go?

5:00 AM	10:00 AM	2:00 PM	4:00 PM	5:00 PM
50	55	68	70	70

Cool all day. Cold this morning.

Pray for God's guidance for what we should do about the work matter.

I love you and I just plain love being with you.

It is like a trip (vacation) just to be by your side.

I love you.

REH

If any of you lacks wisdom, let him ask God,

who gives generously to all without reproach,

and it will be given him.

James 1:5 (ESV)

LONG RANGE:

Pray together for wisdom for yourselves individually and as a couple.

5:00 AM	10:00 AM	2:00 PM	4:00 PM	5:00 PM
48	56	69	72	71

Another Friday.

I can't believe how fast time goes.

As long as it is with you, I am okay.

Let it roll, as we roll through life together.

Love you!

REH

My times are in your hand;

rescue me from the hand of my enemies and from my persecutors!

Psalm 31:15 (ESV)

LONG RANGE:

Do you still hold hands? As you're out and about the next few weeks, make an effort to hold each other's hands whenever possible.

5:00 AM	10:00 AM	2:00 PM	4:00 PM	5:00 PM
64	72	82	82	80

Just to be with you – that is all I want.

I just want you by my side always.

REH

Be strong and courageous.

Do not fear or be in dread of them,

for it is the Lord your God who goes with you.

He will not leave you or forsake you."

Deuteronomy 31:6 (ESV)

LONG RANGE:

When have you noticed your spouse being courageous?

5:00 AM	10:00 AM	2:00 PM	4:00 PM	5:00 PM
59	69	83	85	85

Just

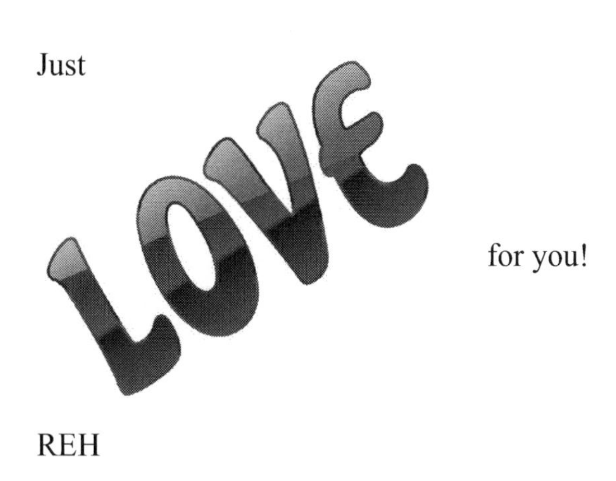

for you!

REH

Jesus said,

"This is my commandment, that you love one another as I have loved you."

John 15:12 (ESV)

LONG RANGE:

Write a simple love note to your spouse.

5:00 AM	10:00 AM	2:00 PM	4:00 PM	5:00 PM
61	68	80	82	82

81 at game time.

Just a little note to say you are my dream girl.

You are all that I need or want.

You and I are one and will always be.

REH

Jesus said,

"So they are no longer two but one flesh.

What therefore God has joined together, let not man separate."

Matthew 19:6 (ESV)

LONG RANGE:

Do you have root for any sports teams? Are you rivals in a house divided or do you cheer on the same teams together? Does your loyalty to a team affect your relationship?

5:00 AM	10:00 AM	2:00 PM	4:00 PM	5:00 PM
57	67	79	81	81

Let my love wrap around you all day today and tomorrow and forever.

I love you.

REH

But you, O Lord, are a shield about me,

my glory, and the lifter of my head.

Psalm 3:3 (ESV)

LONG RANGE:

What do you think "lifter of my head" means in this Psalm? How does God lift your own head?

Just a little note to say I love you.
Brought you something to eat.
See U at Noon.
Love you!
REH

5:00 AM	10:00 AM	2:00 PM	4:00 PM	5:00 PM
69	81	96	97	97

Real hot.

Today is the day God will show us which way we are to go for our major slow down.

It is exciting.

Love you.

Love you being beside me at all times.

REH

Make me to know your ways, O Lord;

teach me your paths.

Lead me in your truth and teach me,

for you are the God of my salvation;

for you I wait all the day long.

Psalm 25:4-5 (ESV)

LONG RANGE:

When was the last time God showed you the direction to take concerning a decision?

5:00 AM	10:00 AM	2:00 PM	4:00 PM	5:00 PM
68	70	80	82	82

Much cooler today.

Next week is our week.

Let us go and enjoy the mountains.

Love to you today and forever.

REH

For behold,

He who forms mountains,

And creates the wind,

Who declares to man what his thought is,

And makes the morning darkness,

Who treads the high places of the earth—

The Lord God of hosts is His name.

Amos 4:13 (NKJV)

LONG RANGE:

Do you have any plans in place to go and enjoy something soon?

5:00 AM	10:00 AM	2:00 PM	4:00 PM	5:00 PM
74	79	87	87	85

Cooler than yesterday.

Thanks for what you said last night.

You know with a capital K that I love you.

U R my dream girl.

U R my everything.

I love you.

REH

Let the words of my mouth and the meditation of my heart

be acceptable in your sight,

O Lord, my rock and my redeemer.

Psalm 19:14 (ESV)

LONG RANGE:

Do your words uplift, encourage, affirm your spouse?

5:00 AM	10:00 AM	2:00 PM	4:00 PM	5:00 PM
70	81	93	94	94

Enjoyed afternoon with you and not working.

Meal was excellent.

Love just being with you, no matter what we are doing.

Ok?

Love you.

REH

Now to him who is able to do far more abundantly than all that we ask or think,

according to the power at work within us,

to him be glory in the church and in Christ Jesus throughout all generations,

forever and ever.

Ephesians 3:20-21 (ESV)

LONG RANGE:

Cook a new recipe together. Then clean the kitchen together.

5:00 AM	10:00 AM	2:00 PM	4:00 PM	5:00 PM
73	77	87	89	89

A little cooler – not much though.

Another week of work has passed.

We will know soon what direction our work will go.

Love you and just love being with you.

You do not have to do a thing but be there with me.

REH

And whatever you do in word or deed, do all in the name of the Lord Jesus,

giving thanks to God the Father through Him.

Colossians 3:17 (NKJV)

LONG RANGE:

What do you do when you don't know what to do?

5:00 AM	10:00 AM	2:00 PM	4:00 PM	5:00 PM
70	72	82	84	85

Just a few days and we are on the road to the mountains.

Just you and me and God.

Oh what a time it will be.

Love you and am ready to GO.

REH

For the Lord is the great God,

And the great King above all gods.

In His hand are the deep places of the earth;

The heights of the hills are His also.

Psalm 95:4-5 (NKJV)

LONG RANGE:

Are you spontaneous or deliberate in your plans together? Are you opposites in that regard?

5:00 AM	10:00 AM	2:00 PM	4:00 PM	5:00 PM
70	80	92	94	93

Wednesday already – time sure moves fast for us.

As long as I am with you that is OK with me.

You make me complete.

You did a wonderful job last night.

You honored God and His glory was seen through you.

Ok. Ok.

REH

Be steadfast, immovable, always abounding in the work of the Lord,

knowing that your labor is not in vain in the Lord.

1 Corinthians 15:58 (NKJV)

LONG RANGE:

Do you sometimes feel like your labor is in vain? Do you feel underappreciated or even ignored?

5:00 AM	10:00 AM	2:00 PM	4:00 PM	5:00 PM
70	81	94	95	94

If I had it to do over again I certainly would.

Without you, I am nothing.

You make me what I am.

I love you.

Always and forever.

REH

And the Lord God formed man of the dust of the ground,

and breathed into his nostrils the breath of life;

and man became a living being.

Genesis 2:7 (NKJV)

LONG RANGE:

If you could do one thing over, what would it be? How would that change who you are today?

5:00 AM	10:00 AM	2:00 PM	4:00 PM	5:00 PM
71	81	93	93	92

7 p.m. 88

Let your light shine for God's glory tonight.

Let the ladies know what God (our God) has done for you.

Love you and stand behind you.

REH

Then Jesus spoke to them again, saying,

"I am the light of the world.

He who follows Me shall not walk in darkness,

but have the light of life."

John 8:12 (NKJV)

LONG RANGE:

Do you have a ministry? Have you ever explored ways that you could touch hearts and change lives?

5:00 AM	10:00 AM	2:00 PM	4:00 PM	5:00 PM
74	78	89	90	90

Warmer today.

Pack tonight.

Tomorrow we head to the mountains.

Just you and me and God.

What a time we shall have!

Love you!

REH

Jesus said,

"If you have faith as a mustard seed, you will say to this mountain,

'Move from here to there,' and it will move;

and nothing will be impossible for you."

Matthew 17:20 (NKJV)

LONG RANGE:

How do you experience God's presence in your daily life?

5:00 AM	10:00 AM	2:00 PM	4:00 PM	5:00 PM
68	76	87	89	89

Our day to travel. Probably cooler in the mountains.

Now is the time you and I have been looking for.

Just you and me and God to see how God leads us in our study for the people.

I love you.

REH

Give instruction to a wise man, and he will be still wiser;

Teach a just man, and he will increase in learning.

Proverbs 9:9 (NKJV)

LONG RANGE:

Do you like driving and exploring in the mountains? What do you like most? Least?

5:00 AM	10:00 AM	2:00 PM	4:00 PM	5:00 PM
70	77	88	90	91

Good to be back home.

Have court this morning. I am up and at 'em.

I love you.

You are ALL I need for anything.

I love you.

REH

I have surely built You an exalted house,

And a place for You to dwell in forever.

1 Kings 8:13 (NKJV)

LONG RANGE:

Do you pray for your spouse's work? Ask each other for specific prayer requests for the coming week, and make that a weekly habit.

5:00 AM	10:00 AM	2:00 PM	4:00 PM	5:00 PM
74	76	83	84	83

Your people want to meet Wed morning, not Tues night. Check messages.

Love that is just for you from me.

I love you!

REH

Therefore comfort each other and edify one another, just as you also are doing.

1 Thessalonians 5:11 (NKJV)

LONG RANGE:

How can your spouse support you this week?

5:00 AM	10:00 AM	2:00 PM	4:00 PM	5:00 PM
73	81	92	93	92

Last day of court for this week.

Can't believe how fast time is moving for us.

My love for you growing as these fast days pass.

It will always and forever be growing to love you more.

REH

Love you

So neither he who plants nor he who waters is anything,

but only God who gives the growth.

1 Corinthians 3:7 (ESV)

LONG RANGE:

Create a heart for your spouse – draw, paint, sculpt, build, sew, cook, etc – use the gifts and skills God gave you to create a tangible expression of your love for each other.

5:00 AM	10:00 AM	2:00 PM	4:00 PM	5:00 PM
75	83	91	91	90

Next week we go to the mountains.

Just you and me.

I love that.

I love you.

REH

All you inhabitants of the world,

you who dwell on the earth,

when a signal is raised on the mountains, look!

When a trumpet is blown, hear!

Isaiah 18:3 (ESV)

LONG RANGE:

Read the book of Revelation, discussing and researching signs of the end times together.

5:00 AM	10:00 AM	2:00 PM	4:00 PM	5:00 PM
74	76	82	83	83

Little cooler today. No 90s.

You make my life complete.

Without you, I am not a whole person.

It is you and me forever and ever.

PTL it is so.

Love you.

REH

For the word of God is living and active, sharper than any two-edged sword,
piercing to the division of soul and of spirit, of joints and of marrow,
and discerning the thoughts and intentions of the heart.
Hebrews 4:12 (ESV)

LONG RANGE:

How is the word of God living and active in your marriage?

5:00 AM	10:00 AM	2:00 PM	4:00 PM	5:00 PM
73	81	90	91	90

E's DAY!

Hot day because you are HOT and it is your day!

I love you more and more as we shelter-in-place (here and at the office).

Love you.

REH

"How beautiful you are, my darling,

How beautiful you are!

Your eyes are like doves."

Song of Solomon 1:15

LONG RANGE:

Have you had to shelter-in-place during the pandemic? What was the most difficult part?

5:00 AM	10:00 AM	2:00 PM	4:00 PM	5:00 PM
72	80	90	92	91

Much warmer than yesterday.

It is not just another day.

It is a day of being with the person you love the most.

It is a good day, come what may.

REH, who loves EHH

The Lord is not slow to fulfill his promise as some count slowness,

but is patient toward you, not wishing that any should perish,

but that all should reach repentance.

2 Peter 3:9 (ESV)

LONG RANGE:

What promises has God fulfilled in your lives?

5:00 AM	10:00 AM	2:00 PM	4:00 PM	5:00 PM
68	77	86	84	84

May rain in the afternoon – 40% chance.

Love just for you this day and every other day that we live and then forever in Heaven.

You and me serving God forever together.

Amen.

I love you.

REH

But now they desire a better, that is, a heavenly country.

Therefore God is not ashamed to be called their God,

for He has prepared a city for them.

Hebrews 11:16 (NKJV)

LONG RANGE:

Together, talk about what you imagine Heaven will be like. Make a plan to read more about Heaven in the Bible and in books.

5:00 AM	10:00 AM	2:00 PM	4:00 PM	5:00 PM
72	75	88	88	88

Your note was awesome.

All you say about me, I say about you.

We are ONE.

We are together and will be always.

We are servants of the God Most High.

We dwell with God.

I love you.

REH

"Do you not know that you are a temple of God
and that the Spirit of God dwells in you?"
1 Corinthians 3:16

LONG RANGE:

Write love notes to each other this week.

5:00 AM	10:00 AM	2:00 PM	4:00 PM	5:00 PM
73	**82**	**93**	**93**	**93**

I love you.

Each day my love for you grows.

I do not see how, but it does.

I love you more each day.

REH

"'Call to Me and I will answer you,
and I will tell you great and mighty things,
which you do not know.'"
Jeremiah 33:3

LONG RANGE:

What's one thing you didn't know about your spouse when you first married that you know and love about them now?

5:00 AM	10:00 AM	2:00 PM	4:00 PM	5:00 PM
70	82	91	88	88

Rain – 50% chance. Cooler late afternoon.

Another week to start.

All is OK with me as long as I am starting with you.

You are my starter.

I love you.

REH

"Therefore, if anyone is in Christ, he is a new creation;

old things have passed away;

behold, all things have become new."

2 Corinthians 5:17

LONG RANGE:

Plan a date for later this week. Doesn't have to be fancy or expensive, unless you want it to be – just make time to flirt with each other and be a couple together.

5:00 AM	10:00 AM	2:00 PM	4:00 PM	5:00 PM
73	82	90	91	90

You R my Dream Girl.

You R SO SPECIAL.

Especially on your B/D tomorrow.

I just love you the way you are.

I love you.

REH

"May He grant you your heart's desire

And fulfill your whole plan!"

Psalm 20:4

LONG RANGE:

How is your spouse your "Dream Mate"? How do you celebrate and recognize your spouse's birthday each year?

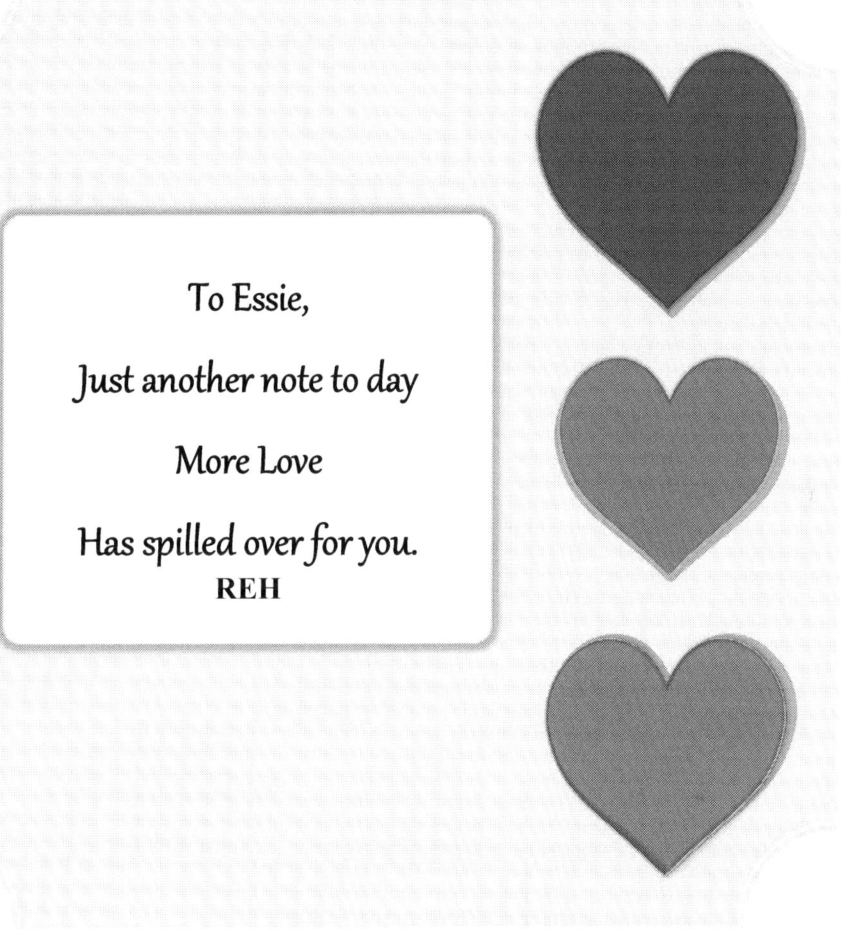
To Essie,
Just another note to day
More Love
Has spilled over for you.
REH

5:00 AM	10:00 AM	2:00 PM	4:00 PM	5:00 PM
72	77	89	89	89

Love rules in our lives.

PTL that is so.

God rules in our lives.

PTL that is so.

Praise God for all He has done for you and me.

Love you.

REH

The Lord has established his throne in the heavens,

and his kingdom rules over all.

Psalm 103:19 (ESV)

LONG RANGE:

How does God rule in your household? Are there areas where you need to let Him rule more?

5:00 AM	10:00 AM	2:00 PM	4:00 PM	5:00 PM
74	82	93	92	91

Praying for your foot to heal.

God can do it.

Hope you feel better this morning.

I love you!

REH

Is anyone among you sick?

Let him call for the elders of the church, and let them pray over him,

anointing him with oil in the name of the Lord.

And the prayer of faith will save the one who is sick,

and the Lord will raise him up.

And if he has committed sins, he will be forgiven.

James 5:14-15 (ESV)

LONG RANGE:

Do you believe God still gives miracles today? Have you ever experienced a miracle yourself, or know someone who has?

5:00 AM	10:00 AM	2:00 PM	4:00 PM	5:00 PM
72	79	88	89	89

Meeting at 5 p.m. today.

Yesterday was a good day.

Today will be even better.

Our Lord is so good to us.

Love you.

REH

Jesus said,

"Therefore do not be anxious about tomorrow,

for tomorrow will be anxious for itself.

Sufficient for the day is its own trouble."

Matthew 6:34 (ESV)

LONG RANGE:

Are you a worrier? What steps can you take to help you worry less? How can your spouse help?

5:00 AM	10:00 AM	2:00 PM	4:00 PM	5:00 PM
73	77	83	83	81

Let us go and worship our mighty God together as always.

Love to you!

REH

Jesus said,

"But the hour is coming, and is now here,

when the true worshipers will worship the Father in spirit and truth,

for the Father is seeking such people to worship him."

John 4:23 (ESV)

LONG RANGE:

Hold hands and pray together, worshiping God in your words and your heart.

5:00 AM	10:00 AM	2:00 PM	4:00 PM	5:00 PM
69	**82**	**90**	**90**	**90**

Love that is for you only.

Love forever and ever, just for you from

REH

I love you!

Jesus said,

"If you love me, you will keep my commandments."

John 14:15 (ESV)

LONG RANGE:

Write "I love you!" on a note for your spouse. Add doodles or more, if you wish.

5:00 AM	10:00 AM	2:00 PM	4:00 PM	5:00 PM
74	83	93	93	93

We are both getting a little better each day.

PTL our God.

Love you.

Love being with you.

Just plain love you.

REH

Earnestly desire the higher gifts.

And I will show you a still more excellent way.

1 Corinthians 12:31 (ESV)

LONG RANGE:

If you don't already know what your spiritual gifts are, explore them and take an assessment that will help you learn what yours are. There are many options online, but here's one for your convenience: https://giftstest.com/ Discuss your gifts with each other and notice the similarities and differences so you can encourage and help each other maximize them all.

5:00 AM	10:00 AM	2:00 PM	4:00 PM	5:00 PM
68	73	83	86	85

Good time with you by my side.

I love you.

I love you being with me at all times.

REH

Keep your life free from love of money, and be content with what you have,

for He has said, "I will never leave you nor forsake you."

Hebrews 13:5 (ESV)

LONG RANGE:

Do you enjoy being together?

5:00 AM	10:00 AM	2:00 PM	4:00 PM	5:00 PM
74	81	92	93	92

Love shall rule.

It is ruling with us.

We are ONE as God has directed.

I love you more each day that I live with you.

REH

LOVE YOU!

Jesus said,

"But from the beginning of creation, 'God made them male and female.'

'Therefore a man shall leave his father and mother and hold fast to his wife,

and the two shall become one flesh.' So they are no longer two but one flesh.

What therefore God has joined together, let not man separate."

Mark 10:6-9 (ESV)

LONG RANGE:

Recall rocky times in your marriage and discuss how God brought you through them. Acknowledge how you've grown and changed because of those times.

5:00 AM	10:00 AM	2:00 PM	4:00 PM	5:00 PM
76	87	94	94	92

You R so SPECIAL.

Do not forget that.

REH

Love to you.

Jesus said,

"You did not choose Me, but I chose you

and appointed you that you should go and bear fruit and that your fruit should abide,

so that whatever you ask the Father in My name,

He may give it to you."

John 15:16 (ESV)

LONG RANGE:

Was it love at first sight for the two of you?

5:00 AM	10:00 AM	2:00 PM	4:00 PM	5:00 PM
74	84	91	90	88

I am ready to go to the beach.

Just love being anywhere if you are there.

Love,

REH, who loves EHH

Jesus said to her, "Everyone who drinks of this water will be thirsty again,
but whoever drinks of the water that I will give him will never be thirsty again.
The water that I will give him will become in him
a spring of water welling up to eternal life."
John 4:13-14 (ESV)

LONG RANGE:

What are you longing for at the moment?

5:00 AM	10:00 AM	2:00 PM	4:00 PM	5:00 PM
78	87	95	96	96

Almost 100.

Nothing here this morning but LOVE.

That is LOVE for YOU!

REH

Therefore with joy you will draw water

From the wells of salvation.

Isaiah 12:3 (NKJV)

LONG RANGE:

Buy a case of bottled water and hand them out to strangers you encounter this week.

5:00 AM	10:00 AM	2:00 PM	4:00 PM	5:00 PM
77	86	94	96	96

Getting close to 100.

I love you more than my words can express.

Just LOVE, LOVE, LOVE and more LOVE.

REH

Pleasant words are like a honeycomb,

Sweetness to the soul and health to the bones.

Proverbs 16:24 (NKJV)

LONG RANGE:

Describe your spouse with positive, pleasant, life-giving, loving words.

5:00 AM	10:00 AM	2:00 PM	4:00 PM	5:00 PM
78	87	95	97	96

Just love being with you no matter where we are.

You + Me – together.

REH

Draw near to God and He will draw near to you.

James 4:8 (NKJV)

LONG RANGE:

What are some ways you can draw nearer to God?

5:00 AM	10:00 AM	2:00 PM	4:00 PM	5:00 PM
77	82	89	90	88

Another week has passed.

However, my love for you does not pass.

It is everlasting.

It is forever. It is always.

It never ends.

REH

Love to EHH

Jesus said,

"He who hears My word and believes in Him who sent Me has everlasting life,

and shall not come into judgement,

but has passed from death into life."

John 5:24 (NKJV)

LONG RANGE:

What does everlasting love mean to you?

5:00 AM	10:00 AM	2:00 PM	4:00 PM	5:00 PM
73	81	86	87	85

Just being with you is a WONDERFUL time and I had a WONDERFUL time last night.

Love to you.

REH

Surely goodness and mercy shall follow me

All the days of my life;

And I will dwell in the house of the Lord

Forever.

Psalm 23:6 (NKJV)

LONG RANGE:

Plan a wonderful night together.

5:00 AM	10:00 AM	2:00 PM	4:00 PM	5:00 PM
74	82	88	89	88

At least not 90.

Love here overflows for you.

It cannot and will not stop.

It grows each day.

Love to EHH

From REH

Mercy, peace, and love be multiplied to you.

Jude 1:2 (NKJV)

LONG RANGE:

Show some mercy this week: get involved in a local ministry for the homeless or the hungry or those in prison.

5:00 AM	10:00 AM	2:00 PM	4:00 PM	5:00 PM
75	84	91	88	88

Just love here for you.

Now and always.

REH

Do not remember the former things,

Nor consider the things of old.

Behold, I will do a new thing,

Now it shall spring forth;

Shall you not know it?

I will even make a road in the wilderness

And rivers in the desert.

Isaiah 43:18-19 (NKJV)

LONG RANGE:

How has God changed you since you made Him Lord of your life?

5:00 AM	10:00 AM	2:00 PM	4:00 PM	5:00 PM
74	83	91	91	90

You are SPECIAL.

Never forget that.

Special to me and to others.

We need you.

REH

Love you!

For You formed my inward parts;

You covered me in my mother's womb.

I will praise You, for I am fearfully and wonderfully made;

Marvelous are Your works,

And that my soul knows very well.

Psalm 139:13-14 (NKJV)

LONG RANGE:

Tell your spouse what makes him/her so special.

5:00 AM	10:00 AM	2:00 PM	4:00 PM	5:00 PM
75	85	93	92	92

Love to you

as it will always be.

Love,

REH

For I am the Lord, I do not change.

Malachi 3:6 (NKJV)

LONG RANGE:

What does it mean to you that the Lord does not change?

5:00 AM	10:00 AM	2:00 PM	4:00 PM	5:00 PM
73	82	90	89	88

There is nothing here but love.

But there is plenty of love from me to you.

Love EHH.

REH

Command those who are rich in this present age not to be haughty,

nor to trust in uncertain riches but in the living God,

who gives us richly all things to enjoy.

Let them do good, that they be rich in good works, ready to give, willing to share,

storing up for themselves a good foundation for the time to come,

that they may lay hold on eternal life.

1 Timothy 6:17-19 (NKJV)

LONG RANGE:

Do you give to others easily? Or is it difficult?

5:00 AM	10:00 AM	2:00 PM	4:00 PM	5:00 PM
44	48	57	58	55

There is only love here for you.

Ok?

Just love.

REH

Jesus said,

"Ask, and it will be given to you;

seek, and you will find;

knock, and it will be opened to you.

For everyone who asks receives, and he who seeks finds,

and to him who knocks it will be opened.

Matthew 7:7-8 (NKJV)

LONG RANGE:

Go stargazing this week.

5:00 AM	10:00 AM	2:00 PM	4:00 PM	5:00 PM
37	48	61	61	59

Cooler today.

Every day is thanksgiving for us!

PTL.

Love you.

Rejoice always, pray without ceasing,

in everything give thanks;

for this is the will of God in Christ Jesus for you.

1 Thessalonians 5:16-18 (NKJV)

LONG RANGE:

Start a Gratitude Jar. Keep a gallon jar somewhere convenient, with some squares of paper or index cards next to it. Add your thanks and gratitude to the jar as you go throughout the year, then read all the cards at Thanksgiving.

5:00 AM	10:00 AM	2:00 PM	4:00 PM	5:00 PM
34	43	48	48	48

Can't hardly take in how good God is to us.

PTL PTL PTL.

We are so blessed.

Thank God for it.

I love you!

REH

Do you despise the riches of His goodness, forbearance, and longsuffering,

not knowing that the goodness of God leads you to repentance?

Romans 2:4 (NKJV)

LONG RANGE:

How has God blessed you this year?

5:00 AM	10:00 AM	2:00 PM	4:00 PM	5:00 PM
41	44	51	53	53

Cool today and cloudy.

Home sweet home.

There is no place like home with you.

I love you.

I am rested up.

Love to Essie

From REH

I will both lie down in peace, and sleep;

For You alone, O Lord, make me dwell in safety.

Psalm 4:8 (NKJV)

LONG RANGE:

What makes your home so sweet?

5:00 AM	10:00 AM	2:00 PM	4:00 PM	5:00 PM
38	48	61	63	62

Warmer. Sunshine.

Nothing but LOVE here for you.

You looked so beautiful last night.

Keep it up.

I love you, and I love the way you look.

REH

You will also be a crown of beauty in the hand of the Lord,

And a royal headband in the hand of your God.

Isaiah 62:3

LONG RANGE:

Husbands, express your wife's beauty in word, written or spoken.

5:00 AM	10:00 AM	2:00 PM	4:00 PM	5:00 PM
43	54	72	73	72

Another week.

Start the week and keep the week with love.

Let God rule and all things will be in place.

I love / I love being with you.

REH

Owe nothing to anyone except to love one another;

for the one who loves his neighbor has fulfilled the Law.

Romans 13:8

LONG RANGE:

Plan to share some love-in-action with one of your neighbors this week. (Examples: provide a meal or bake them some bread or cookies; mow their lawn; take them some flowers or a potted plant; give them a banner for their garden.)

5:00 AM	10:00 AM	2:00 PM	4:00 PM	5:00 PM
53	58	69	79	69

Warm and cloudy.

I am ready for the beach now.

I just love being with you – anywhere, anytime.

I love you more and more each day.

REH

Jesus said,

"Blessed are the peacemakers, for they will be called sons of God."

Matthew 5:9

LONG RANGE:

Who's the peacemaker in your family?

5:00 AM	10:00 AM	2:00 PM	4:00 PM	5:00 PM
41	47	55	55	54

Cloudy.

Today just serve God and all will be okay.

I love you.

I love being with you.

REH

Serve the Lord with fear,

And rejoice with trembling.

Psalm 2:11 (NKJV)

LONG RANGE:

How will you serve God this week?

5:00 AM	10:00 AM	2:00 PM	4:00 PM	5:00 PM
37	47	61	62	60

Without love,

Life is meaningless.

Oh! How I love YOU!

Just love being by your side – ALWAYS.

REH

I have shown you in every way, by laboring like this,

that you must support the weak.

And remember the words of the Lord Jesus, that He said,

'It is more blessed to give than to receive.'

Acts 20:35 (NJKV)

LONG RANGE:

Are you aware of the weak around you? Elderly, sick, frail, homeless, hungry? Notice them, then support them this week.

5:00 AM	10:00 AM	2:00 PM	4:00 PM	5:00 PM
59	63	67	66	65

Warm. 40% chance of rain.

Not much storm for us.

PTL PTL.

Let us go and worship our God!

Oh! How I love you and love being with you no matter what we are doing.

REH

He calms the storm,

So that its waves are still.

Psalm 107:29 (NKJV)

LONG RANGE:

Are you prepared for storms this year? Work on plans to make you more prepared.

5:00 AM	10:00 AM	2:00 PM	4:00 PM	5:00 PM
66	68	73	73	73

High winds. Warm. 50% rain.

Eye will be better today; you can count on it.

Love you and it hurts me to see you in pain.

Okay – you R my love now and forever.

REH

Therefore let those who suffer according to the will of God
commit their souls to Him in doing good,
as to a faithful Creator.
1 Peter 4:19 (NKJV)

LONG RANGE:

What feelings do you experience when your spouse is sick or in pain? Do you worry? Fear? Hurt?

LONG RANGE:

Take turns providing breakfast for your spouse this week.

5:00 AM	10:00 AM	2:00 PM	4:00 PM	5:00 PM
28	37	50	52	50

Cold all day.

You R better but not well.

Keep on getting better.

You will get there.

It hurts me to see you sick.

I love you so much.

You mean everything to me.

REH

He will wipe away every tear from their eyes, and death shall be no more,

neither shall there be mourning, nor crying, nor pain anymore,

for the former things have passed away.

Revelation 21:4 (ESV)

LONG RANGE:

Talk about this Bible verse and what it means to you personally.

5:00 AM	10:00 AM	2:00 PM	4:00 PM	5:00 PM
41	42	52	54	54

Slightly warmer, but not much.

Only to office if you feel like it, okay?

You must do whatever to take care of you.

I need you too much in my life.

I love you!

REH

For I will restore health to you,

and your wounds I will heal,

declares the Lord,

Jeremiah 30:17 (ESV)

LONG RANGE:

Is it difficult for you to rest? To take care of yourself? What are some ways you can do better?

5:00 AM	10:00 AM	2:00 PM	4:00 PM	5:00 PM
43	47	59	61	60

Cloudy, cool all day.

PTL, I can tell you R getting better.

It hurts me to see you hurt.

I love you so.

You are my BFF.

Love,

REH

He heals the brokenhearted

and binds up their wounds.

Psalm 147:3 (ESV)

LONG RANGE:

When was the last time your heart was broken? How has it healed?

5:00 AM	10:00 AM	2:00 PM	4:00 PM	5:00 PM
56	49	51	52	50

Cold all day, rain.

You will be well soon.

Hang in there.

Keep believing. Keep trusting.

You R my BFF.

You will always be my BFF.

REH

For with the heart one believes and is justified,

and with the mouth one confesses and is saved.

Romans 10:10 (ESV)

LONG RANGE:

Was it hard or easy to learn to trust your spouse? What helps build that trust?

5:00 AM	10:00 AM	2:00 PM	4:00 PM	5:00 PM
59	46	48	46	45

Cold all day.

48 high – freezing per grandson, because it's lower than 50.

Not freezing but still cold.

Dress warm.

You know I can always keep you warm.

Two are better than one.

We 2 are 1. Amen.

I love you.

REH

Two are better than one,

Because they have a good reward for their labor.

Ecclesiastes 4:9 (NKJV)

LONG RANGE:

How does "two are better than one" play a role in your marriage?

5:00 AM	10:00 AM	2:00 PM	4:00 PM	5:00 PM
28	37	46	48	46

Cold all day.

Packing tonight.

Ready for tomorrow.

Can't wait.

Mtns here we come.

Train here we come.

Love you and love being with you no matter where we are.

REH

How beautiful upon the mountains
are the feet of him who brings good news,
who publishes peace, who brings good news of happiness,
who publishes salvation,
who says to Zion, "Your God reigns."
Isaiah 52:7 (ESV)

LONG RANGE:

Have you ever ridden on a train? If not, is that on your bucket list?

5:00 AM	10:00 AM	2:00 PM	4:00 PM	5:00 PM
39	52	62	63	61

Game time. Good time with part of your family here.

Today we see some other parts of your family.

You are blessed.

You are covered.

Esp by REH

REH

Jesus said,

"Whoever does the will of My Father who is in heaven,

he is My brother, and sister, and mother."

Matthew 12:50

LONG RANGE:

Do you have family gatherings? Are they fun or stressful?

5:00 AM	10:00 AM	2:00 PM	4:00 PM	5:00 PM
31	36	45	46	45

Cold all day.

U R Better.

I can tell by the way you move.

Love you.

Love you being better.

REH

You shall serve the Lord your God, and he will bless your bread and your water,

and I will take sickness away from among you.

Exodus 23:25 (ESV)

LONG RANGE:

Are you an introvert or an extrovert? How does that play a role in your marriage and family life? (If you've never taken a personality test, you can take a free one here: https://www.16personalities.com/free-personality-test)

5:00 AM	10:00 AM	2:00 PM	4:00 PM	5:00 PM
27	36	43	44	43

Real cold all day. (Eye doc at 11:30 today)

Maybe you should stay in today. It is real cold all day.

This message is from the one who loves you and is trying to take care of you.

I want you secure at all times.

I love you and will always.

We R One.

REH

But let all who take refuge in you rejoice;

let them ever sing for joy,

and spread your protection over them,

that those who love your name may exult in you.

Psalm 5:11 (ESV)

LONG RANGE:

Write your spouse a note that will encourage them throughout the day.

5:00 AM	10:00 AM	2:00 PM	4:00 PM	5:00 PM
34	39	51	53	52

Cold and cloudy all day.

The Lord's Day.

Glad U R Home.

Take care of yourself.

I need and want you so much.

You R my life.

You make me complete.

I love you.

REH

Remember the Sabbath day, to keep it holy.

Six days you shall labor, and do all your work,

but the seventh day is a Sabbath to the Lord your God.

Exodus 20:8-10 (ESV)

LONG RANGE:

What are some ways you would like to keep the Sabbath holy in your own home?

5:00 AM	10:00 AM	2:00 PM	4:00 PM	5:00 PM
45	46	52	53	52

Another week starting with the one person I want to start it with.

So glad you are better.

I love you.

I always want to be near you.

You are my partner-in-life.

Love just for you.

REH

So God created man in his own image,

in the image of God he created him;

male and female he created them.

Genesis 1:27 (ESV)

LONG RANGE:

Imagine God's image. How would you describe Him?

5:00 AM	10:00 AM	2:00 PM	4:00 PM	5:00 PM
61	63	70	70	70

Love just for you.

Every day my love for you grows.

Okay?

You R my dream girl.

You R the 1.

REH

Whatever is true, whatever is honorable, whatever is just,
whatever is pure, whatever is lovely, whatever is commendable,
if there is any excellence, if there is anything worthy of praise,
think about these things.
Philippians 4:8 (ESV)

LONG RANGE:

Send your spouse a love text or write them a love note using "text-speak" abbreviations.

5:00 AM	10:00 AM	2:00 PM	4:00 PM	5:00 PM
39	46	59	59	58

Day of travel.

I am READY.

I am so glad you are better.

I love you soooo.

I am looking forward to our little trip.

We (you and me) need it.

Love shall always rule in our lives.

We belong to God and each other.

I love you.

REH

Jesus said,

"They will come from the east and the west, from the north and the south,

and sit down in the kingdom of God."

Luke 13:29 (NKJV)

LONG RANGE:

What are you looking forward to right now?

5:00 AM	10:00 AM	2:00 PM	4:00 PM	5:00 PM
50	50	56	56	57

Cloudy.

Another week starting.

It is all okay as long as you start it with me.

Okay?

I love you.

And I love being with you.

REH

He has made everything beautiful in its time.

Also He has put eternity in their hearts,

except that no one can find out the work that God does from beginning to end.

Ecclesiastes 3:11 (NKJV)

LONG RANGE:

Describe something beautiful you've seen lately. Give God the thanks for His creation.

5:00 AM	10:00 AM	2:00 PM	4:00 PM	5:00 PM
45	46	48	50	50

Cold all day. May rain.

Home with you.

Every time I am with you, I am home.

That is where my home is (where you are).

I just want to be with you.

I love you.

REH

Now My eyes will be open and My ears attentive to prayer made in this place.

2 Chronicles 7:15 (NKJV)

LONG RANGE:

How has your home changed during your marriage?

5:00 AM	10:00 AM	2:00 PM	4:00 PM	5:00 PM
66	68	81	82	82

Hotter today.

God is blessing you and me so much.

You make me complete.

Without you, I am not a whole person.

I love you and just love being with you.

REH

After you have suffered for a little while, the God of all grace,

who called you to His eternal glory in Christ,

will Himself perfect, confirm, strengthen, and establish you.

1 Peter 5:10

LONG RANGE:

What are some of the ways you've suffered in life? How did you get through those times?

5:00 AM	10:00 AM	2:00 PM	4:00 PM	5:00 PM
41	48	61	61	57

Cold all day.

Keep doing as you are.

You look so good and I can tell you are getting better each day. I just love saying that.

I also love saying,

I love you.

I love being with you.

I just plain love you.

REH

PTL for He is good to us.

Praise the Lord, all nations!

Extol him, all peoples!

For great is his steadfast love toward us,

and the faithfulness of the Lord endures forever.

Praise the Lord!

Psalm 117: 1-2 (ESV)

LONG RANGE:

Write a note of encouragement to your spouse.

5:00 AM	10:00 AM	2:00 PM	4:00 PM	5:00 PM
45	57	66	64	61

Cold all day.

Remember my love for you is always growing.

You make my life complete.

You are my DREAM GIRL.

You are all I need or want.

You are it. So be it.

I love you more as we grow older together.

REH

Gray hair is a crown of glory;

it is gained in a righteous life.

Proverbs 16:31 (ESV)

LONG RANGE:

How has age, and aging, played a role in your marriage?

5:00 AM	10:00 AM	2:00 PM	4:00 PM	5:00 PM
36	42	56	59	59

Cold all day.

REH loves you and always will.

We are and shall be ONE.

REH

But he who is joined to the Lord becomes one spirit with him.

1 Corinthians 6:17 (ESV)

LONG RANGE:

Do you always feel as one in your marriage? Or are there times when you feel the exact opposite? How do you deal with those times?

5:00 AM	10:00 AM	2:00 PM	4:00 PM	5:00 PM
53	56	64	63	61

Trip with you absolutely great.

Being home with you is better.

I love you and I love being with you.

Why??

'Cause I love you.

REH

Jesus said,

"For life is more than food, and the body more than clothing."

Luke 12:23 (ESV)

LONG RANGE:

What excites you most about your marriage?

5:00 AM	10:00 AM	2:00 PM	4:00 PM	5:00 PM
37	40	45	46	46

Our day to go.

46 high for home; cooler where we R going.

I am ready to go anywhere as long as you are with me.

I love you.

Truly.

REH

Jesus said,

"Go therefore and make disciples of all the nations,

baptizing them in the name of the Father and of the Son and of the Holy Spirit,

teaching them to observe all things that I have commanded you;

and lo, I am with you always, even to the end of the age."

Matthew 28:19-20 (NKJV)

LONG RANGE:

Have you ever witnessed to anyone? How did they respond? Do you find it difficult or easy?

5:00 AM	10:00 AM	2:00 PM	4:00 PM	5:00 PM
44	55	68	68	66

Warmer. Okay!

Another week gone by.

Life is but a vapor, per God's word.

So true.

Life is SPECIAL when you have someone SPECIAL like you to share life with.

Love you.

REH

Jesus said,

"You are the light of the world. A city that is set on a hill cannot be hidden.

Nor do they light a lamp and put it under a basket, but on a lampstand,

and it gives light to all who are in the house.

Let your light so shine before men, that they may see your good works

and glorify your Father in heaven."

Matthew 5:14-16 (NKJV)

LONG RANGE:

Do you have a Christian testimony of when/how you were saved? Or perhaps some other significant event in your walk with the Lord? Write it down, then share it with each other.

5:00 AM	10:00 AM	2:00 PM	4:00 PM	5:00 PM
59	63	70	67	66

Just you and me together forever.

This is what God has planned for us.

It will be so.

Amen.

REH loves EHH

A man's heart plans his way,

But the Lord directs his steps.

Proverbs 16:9 (NKJV)

LONG RANGE:

How do you see God's hand in your marriage? How is life different than you imagined it would be? Is it because of His guidance?

5:00 AM	10:00 AM	2:00 PM	4:00 PM	5:00 PM
58	58	63	62	60

Cold all day.

Praying and waiting, but no word to me.

I love you and am ready to go SOMEWHERE with you.

REH

I wait for the Lord, my soul waits,

And in His word I do hope.

Psalm 130:5 (NKJV)

LONG RANGE:

Is waiting easier or more difficult for you than when you first married? How has it changed?

5:00 AM	10:00 AM	2:00 PM	4:00 PM	5:00 PM
39	47	56	57	55

Just love here for you.

I am ready to go.

Where???

I don't know but I am still ready.

Love you.

REH

Be of the same mind toward one another.

Do not set your mind on high things, but associate with the humble.

Do not be wise in your own opinion.

Romans 12:16 (NKJV)

LONG RANGE:

What does that first line of the verse mean to you? What does it mean to be of the same mind toward one another?

5:00 AM	10:00 AM	2:00 PM	4:00 PM	5:00 PM
43	53	63	63	62

Cloudy, no rain.

Oh! How I love you!!

So much!

REH

Just always be by my side.

REH

For the Lord is good;

his steadfast love endures forever,

and his faithfulness to all generations.

Psalm 100:5 (ESV)

LONG RANGE:

Discuss your wants and needs of marriage. Are you meeting each other's needs?

5:00 AM	10:00 AM	2:00 PM	4:00 PM	5:00 PM
53	60	67	67	66

A little warmer.

I am sorry for all my wrongs against you.

I am working on myself and I have a lot of work to do.

Love you more than ever before and always will.

REH

Therefore, my beloved, as you have always obeyed,

so now, not only as in my presence but much more in my absence,

work out your own salvation with fear and trembling,

for it is God who works in you,

both to will and to work for his good pleasure.

Philippians 2:12-13 (ESV)

LONG RANGE:

What are some ways you need to work on yourself? Pray together and seek the Lord's help.

5:00 AM	10:00 AM	2:00 PM	4:00 PM	5:00 PM
50	61	73	73	71

A little warmer. Sunshine!

Ps. 40:1 is what God has said to me,

“I waited patiently for the Lord and he inclined unto me and heard my cry.”

Let us do so and wait for God.

Love to you, REH

I waited patiently for the Lord;

he inclined to me and heard my cry.

He drew me up from the pit of destruction,

out of the miry bog,

and set my feet upon a rock,

making my steps secure.

He put a new song in my mouth,

a song of praise to our God.

Many will see and fear,

and put their trust in the Lord.

Psalm 40:1-3 (ESV)

LONG RANGE:

Name some of the prayers God has answered for you.

5:00 AM	10:00 AM	2:00 PM	4:00 PM	5:00 PM
57	63	71	71	70

Like yesterday.

Keep waiting.

Keep loving.

Keep trusting.

And all will go well.

Love to you from

REH

The Lord is my strength and my shield;

in him my heart trusts, and I am helped;

my heart exults,

and with my song I give thanks to him.

Psalm 28:7 (ESV)

LONG RANGE:

What does it mean to trust God? Do you trust Him with all areas of your life?

5:00 AM	10:00 AM	2:00 PM	4:00 PM	5:00 PM
38	47	62	64	62

Cool all day.

Another week down.

Another month started.

It is all okay with me as you are with me during time passing so fast.

Love you.

Especially you.

REH

Commit your way to the Lord;

trust in him, and He will act.

Psalm 37:5 (ESV)

LONG RANGE:

Pray together and commit your ways to the Lord.

5:00 AM	10:00 AM	2:00 PM	4:00 PM	5:00 PM
57	64	73	73	73

No fever this morning.

PTL our LORD for He will care for us.

I love you!

Take care of yourself!

REH

Do not fear, for I am with you;

Do not be afraid, for I am your God.

I will strengthen you, I will also help you,

I will also uphold you with My righteous right hand.

Isaiah 41:10

LONG RANGE:

How can you cultivate intimacy in your marriage?

5:00 AM	10:00 AM	2:00 PM	4:00 PM	5:00 PM
55	63	75	79	79

Oh! Just to be with you!

I miss you SOOOOOOO much.

I love you and just plain love being with you – wherever you are.

REH

You will make known to me the way of life;

In Your presence is fullness of joy;

In Your right hand there are pleasures forever.

Psalm 16:11

LONG RANGE:

Is communicating with your spouse difficult or easy? What could make communicating easier?

Are you familiar with ***The 5 Love Languages***? Do you know which ones each of you have?

You can take a free quiz on their website: https://www.5lovelanguages.com/quizzes/

The 5 Love Languages include:

- Receiving Gifts
- Words of Affirmation
- Acts of Service
- Physical Touch
- Quality Time

You can learn more about each language in the book ***The 5 Love Languages*** by Gary Chapman, and on their website, www.5lovelanguages.com

LONG RANGE:

Spend some time discussing and exploring your own love languages and how those languages come into play within your own marriage.

5:00 AM	10:00 AM	2:00 PM	4:00 PM	5:00 PM
57	66	79	81	81

Oh! How I miss you.

I just want to be where you are.

Hospital or wherever, as long as I am with you.

I love you.

I miss you.

REH

The Lord will sustain him upon his sickbed;

In his illness, You restore him to health.

Psalm 41:3

LONG RANGE:

Do you have any hobbies that you do together? Would you be interested in starting one?

5:00 AM	10:00 AM	2:00 PM	4:00 PM	5:00 PM
63	70	79	81	79

Cloudy.

I miss you so much.

You make my life complete.

You make me want to go and do.

You make me.

I love you and I trust OUR GOD to take care of you.

LOVE LOVE LOVE you.

REH

If God be for us, who can be against us?

REH

If God is for us, who is against us?

Romans 8:31

LONG RANGE:

Are you emotionally healthy? Together, explore this Emotional Wellness Toolkit from the National Institute of Health: https://www.nih.gov/health-information/emotional-wellness-toolkit.

5:00 AM	10:00 AM	2:00 PM	4:00 PM	5:00 PM
64	70	79	79	79

Cloudy

Another morning without you and I just cannot stand it.

I MISS YOU SO.

I love you and just want to be with you wherever you are.

REH

But as for me, I will sing of Your strength;

Yes, I will joyfully sing of Your faithfulness in the morning,

For You have been my refuge

And a place of refuge on the day of my distress.

Psalm 59:16

LONG RANGE:

Is your mental health affected by seasons or by the pandemic? How do you work through it?

5:00 AM	10:00 AM	2:00 PM	4:00 PM	5:00 PM
64	72	81	81	81

If you do not come home soon – I am going to stay with you at the hospital.

I cannot bear being without you.

I love and miss you so.

You are my dream girl.

I love you.

REH

How beautiful is your love, my sister, my bride!

How much sweeter is your love than wine,

And the fragrance of your oils

Than that of all kinds of balsam oils!

Song of Solomon 4:10

LONG RANGE:

Has one or either of you been hospitalized before? What was it like being separated for that?

5:00 AM	10:00 AM	2:00 PM	4:00 PM	5:00 PM
46	57	68	70	70

Note says I miss you.

I want to be with you.

I love you more than ever.

God is with you and me forever.

REH

I love Essie.

Set your minds on the things that are above,

not on the things that are on earth.

Colossians 3:2

LONG RANGE:

What does this verse mean to you personally?

5:00 AM	10:00 AM	2:00 PM	4:00 PM	5:00 PM
50	57	72	73	73

Note is here, whether you are or not.

I love you.

I want to be with you.

I miss you.

REH

Give thanks to the God of heaven,

for his steadfast love endures forever.

Psalm 136:26 (ESV)

LONG RANGE:

What's the greatest loss you've experienced during your marriage? How did you grieve?

5:00 AM	10:00 AM	2:00 PM	4:00 PM	5:00 PM
68	68	72	73	73

Cloudy. Cooler today.

Day 3 of quarantine.

You are doing well and I am so glad.

I love you and God certainly will take good care of us both.

In GOD we trust – that is whatever.

I love you.

REH

And those who know your name put their trust in you,

for you, O Lord, have not forsaken those who seek you.

Psalm 9:10 (ESV)

LONG RANGE:

How are you trusting God to take care of you right now?

5:00 AM	10:00 AM	2:00 PM	4:00 PM	5:00 PM
72	75	81	81	77

Hot. 70% chance of rain today.

You are much better. It is visible to me.

PTL PTL for he is so good to us.

I love you so much.

Keep doing as you are, and you will get better as each day passes.

I love you.

REH

Heal me, Lord, and I will be healed;

Save me and I will be saved,

For You are my praise.

Jeremiah 17:14

LONG RANGE:

Pray for any veterans that you know, thanking God for them and for their service, and asking His protection and blessing upon them all. Consider blessing a veteran with a phone call, meal, or small gift this week as a way of saying thanks.

5:00 AM	10:00 AM	2:00 PM	4:00 PM	5:00 PM
57	61	72	73	73

About like yesterday. Cloudy.

Just love.

That is all that is about.

Love and you and me.

Under our God forever.

I love you.

REH

Keep yourselves in the love of God,

waiting for the mercy of our Lord Jesus Christ

that leads to eternal life.

Jude 1:21 (ESV)

LONG RANGE:

Write a weather poem or letter about your marriage.

5:00 AM	10:00 AM	2:00 PM	4:00 PM	5:00 PM
70	73	81	81	81

Rain today. 40% chance in afternoon.

5th day of quarantine.

You are doing great.

Keep it up.

Keep doing as you are.

You will/and are getting better – I can tell.

PTL.

I love you and just plain love being with you – even in quarantine.

LOVE LOVE LOVE.

REH

Two are better than one because they have a good return for their labor;

for if either of them falls, the one will lift up his companion.

Ecclesiastes 4:9-10

LONG RANGE:

How do you lift up your spouse?

5:00 AM	10:00 AM	2:00 PM	4:00 PM	5:00 PM
77	77	81	81	79

Rain this morning; 40% chance this afternoon.

Oh! Thank GOD you are better. I can tell.

You are getting better each day. Keep it up. Keep doing what you are doing.

God is here and will take care of us.

PTL.

I love you!

Also, I am very very much better and know it.

I love you.

REH

We also celebrate in our tribulations, knowing that tribulation brings about perseverance;

and perseverance, proven character; and proven character, hope;

and hope does not disappoint,

because the love of God has been poured out within our hearts

through the Holy Spirit who was given to us.

Romans 5:3-5

LONG RANGE:

What did you celebrate last? If you had to throw a celebration party today, what would you celebrate? What tributions could you celebrate and how would you do it?

5:00 AM	10:00 AM	2:00 PM	4:00 PM	5:00 PM
48	55	66	66	66

Cool all day.

Day 7 of quarantine.

You look good and you are getting better each day – I can tell.

(By the way – I am too.)

I love you and will always love you.

You are everything to me.

Love,

REH

Let endurance have its perfect result,

so that you may be perfect and complete, lacking in nothing.

James 1:4

LONG RANGE:

Meditate on the verse above. How does it speak to you?

5:00 AM	10:00 AM	2:00 PM	4:00 PM	5:00 PM
48	54	64	66	66

Cool all day.

Day 8 of quarantine.

Your time is moving on. Next Saturday will be your last day.

I am so proud of you and how you are doing.

God is with us all the way, all the day.

I just love you more as I stay with you more.

REH

The Lord your God is in your midst,

A victorious warrior.

He will rejoice over you with joy,

He will be quiet in His love,

He will rejoice over you with shouts of joy.

Zephaniah 3:17

LONG RANGE:

Do you consider yourself a prayer warrior?

5:00 AM	10:00 AM	2:00 PM	4:00 PM	5:00 PM
55	63	72	72	70

Day 9 of quarantine.

Time is moving.

You will be out next Sunday. Saturday is your 15th day since leaving hospital.

I love you.

I love caring for you.

I love being with you.

I love everything about you.

I just plain love you.

PTL for our lives together.

REH

Bear one another's burdens, and so fulfill the law of Christ.

Ephesians 6:2 (ESV)

LONG RANGE:

How can you bear your spouse's burdens this week?

5:00 AM	10:00 AM	2:00 PM	4:00 PM	5:00 PM
43	48	59	61	57

Cold all day.

10th day of quarantine.

Only 5 more days.

Keep it up and you will be up.

God has blessed us both tremendously.

I love you and always will.

It seems I love you more each day.

REH

It is my prayer that your love may abound more and more,

with knowledge and all discernment,

so that you may approve what is excellent,

and so be pure and blameless for the day of Christ,

filled with the fruit of righteousness that comes through Jesus Christ,

to the glory and praise of God.

Philippians 1:9-11

LONG RANGE:

How did/does purity play a role in your relationship before you were married and now?

5:00 AM	10:00 AM	2:00 PM	4:00 PM	5:00 PM
36	54	66	66	64

I love you.

Cold all day.

11th day of quarantine.

You are doing so well.

Be patient. Your strength will return.

Soon you will be going, going, and going more.

God has blessed us.

We (our times) are in His hands.

God always works for the Good of us.

Remember that as you consider our options.

REH

But if we hope for what we do not see, we wait for it with patience.

Romans 8:25 (ESV)

LONG RANGE:

What are you hoping for that you cannot see?

5:00 AM	10:00 AM	2:00 PM	4:00 PM	5:00 PM
41	57	70	70	66

Warmer than yesterday.

12th day of quarantine.

Keep on doing as you are.

You are getting better each day. (I can see it.)

I love you and I love being with you.

PTL for his blessings.

He is pouring out on us.

I love you so.

God is with us.

Who can be against us?

REH

Taste and see that the Lord is good;

How blessed is the man who takes refuge in Him!

Psalm 34:8

LONG RANGE:

Surprise your spouse with a special meal this week.

5:00 AM	10:00 AM	2:00 PM	4:00 PM	5:00 PM
45	61	73	73	72

13th day of quarantine.

God has blessed us abundantly.

Let us PTL.

I am so thankful that you are recovering.

I love you and always will.

You make my life complete.

LOVE LOVE LOVE to you.

REH

Is anyone among you suffering? Then he must pray.

Is anyone cheerful? He is to sing praises.

James 5:13

LONG RANGE:

Pray for friends and family you know who are suffering. Give God the praise and glory for those who are doing well.

5:00 AM	10:00 AM	2:00 PM	4:00 PM	5:00 PM
57	64	75	75	73

Not as cold; cloudy.

14th day of Quarantine.

1 more to go.

I am so proud of you and the way you are doing.

God is with us.

God will keep us.

We shall ALWAYS be with each other.

I love you.

REH

For this reason I also suffer these things; but I am not ashamed,
for I know whom I have believed, and I am convinced that He is able
to protect what I have entrusted to Him until that day.
2 Timothy 1:12

LONG RANGE:

Do you suffer when your spouse does?

5:00 AM	10:00 AM	2:00 PM	4:00 PM	5:00 PM
43	50	62	62	60

The best part about my birthday is that you are in it.

That is what counts.

That is what makes the difference.

Love you.

REH

B/D Boy

For by me your days will be multiplied,

and years will be added to your life.

Proverbs 9:11 (ESV)

LONG RANGE:

How do you celebrate each other's birthdays? How do you want to celebrate your next birthday?

5:00 AM	10:00 AM	2:00 PM	4:00 PM	5:00 PM
64	70	81	79	77

Rain in afternoon.

At Home. PTL.

Home sweet home.

It is much sweeter with you here.

PTL.

I love you and am so glad you are home.

Love, Love, and More Love.

REH

My people will abide in a peaceful habitation,

in secure dwellings, and in quiet resting places.

Isaiah 32:18 (ESV)

LONG RANGE:

Could your home be more secure?

6:00 AM	10:00 AM	2:00 PM	4:00 PM	5:00 PM
70	70	77	77	77

About the same from now – all day.

So glad you are home.

So glad you are home with me.

So glad I am home with you.

I love you and just love being with you – wherever.

God is so good to us even with CV-19.

God is still there and caring for us.

PTL.

I love you.

REH

But Jesus said to him, "Why do you call Me good?

No one is good except God alone."

Luke 18:19

LONG RANGE:

How have you seen or experienced God's goodness during the pandemic?

6 am 54

10 am 59

2 pm 70 "cloudy"

4 pm 72

5 pm 73

Need to be thinking about
our next trip. I am ready
to go.
We are doing so good at the
ofc. Cannot do w/o you.
I love you so. You make
it all OK just being there.
I love you.
PTL our God who Loves
us & protects us

KH

5:00 AM	10:00 AM	2:00 PM	4:00 PM	5:00 PM
45	55	64	64	63

Cool all day, especially this morning.

Today is the day.

Remember, only do (work) as your body allows.

Need rest, get rest.

Suggest you take pillow and blanket with you.

I love you and am so proud of you.

God is just great to us.

PTL.

I love you so.

We shall serve GOD together.

REH

"But as for me and my house, we will serve the Lord."

Joshua 24:15

LONG RANGE:

How does your family serve the Lord together? The holiday season is a great time to adopt a needy family, volunteer in a food drive, or donate to a food bank or homeless shelter.

5:00 AM	10:00 AM	2:00 PM	4:00 PM	5:00 PM
75	75	82	82	82

Does not go up but 7 degrees, 75-82.

So glad you and I are better physically.

God is so good to us.

I thank God every day for you.

I love you.

REH

I thank my God always when I remember you in my prayers,

because I hear of your love and of the faith that you have

toward the Lord Jesus and for all the saints.

Philemon 1:4-5

LONG RANGE:

Has God ever brought someone randomly to mind? Do you pray for them? Think of someone recently who came to mind and say a special prayer for them now.

5:00 AM	10:00 AM	2:00 PM	4:00 PM	5:00 PM
63	66	75	79	77

God is so good to us.

PTL for our blessings.

I love you and you and I will serve the Lord together, forever.

I love you and just plain love being with you.

REH

But if we walk in the light, as he is in the light,

we have fellowship with one another,

and the blood of Jesus his Son cleanses us from all sin.

1 John 1:7

LONG RANGE:

Pray together and ask God to forgive you of all your sins, cleanse you of all unrighteousness, and to wash you clean. Thank Him for His sacrifice and His love.

5:00 AM	10:00 AM	2:00 PM	4:00 PM	5:00 PM
64	70	79	79	77

Each day is a wonderful event because of you.

You make me complete.

I love you all the time.

REH

Every word of God is pure;

He is a shield to those who take refuge in Him.

Proverbs 30:5

LONG RANGE:

Rate your marriage on a scale of one to ten. In what areas are you excelling? Which areas need improvement?

5:00 AM	10:00 AM	2:00 PM	4:00 PM	5:00 PM
55	63	72	72	72

Cooler today.

Feeling much better.

Took a shower when I got up.

I love you and love the way you take care of me.

UR the BEST.

REH

Do not let kindness and truth leave you;

Bind them around your neck,

Write them on the tablet of your heart.

Proverbs 3:3

LONG RANGE:

Write your spouse a love note from the tablet of your heart.

5:00 AM	10:00 AM	2:00 PM	4:00 PM	5:00 PM
43	55	70	70	66

Today is the day.

We (you and me) have been practicing law for more than 50 years. We started October 19, 1970 – we are now on year 51 (one month already down.)

I just love you and love you being with me.

So glad you are better.

God is good, let us PTL.

PTL and serve Him.

I love you.

REH

The Lord is good to all,

And His mercies are over all His works.

Psalm 145:9

LONG RANGE:

What anniversaries in your personal and professional lives can you celebrate this year?

5:00 AM	10:00 AM	2:00 PM	4:00 PM	5:00 PM
50	61	72	73	73

Much better on the recovery road.

PTL for His blessings to us.

PTL for you being in my life.

I love you.

REH

For the Lord God is a sun and shield;
the Lord bestows favor and honor.
No good thing does he withhold
from those who walk uprightly.
Psalm 84:11

LONG RANGE:

How and from what does God shield you?

5:00 AM	10:00 AM	2:00 PM	4:00 PM	5:00 PM
72	68	70	68	66

Cloudy and cooler today.

So glad you are BETTER.

So glad you are with me.

So glad you work with me.

So glad you are my wife.

Looks like you make me so glad.

I love you and I am glad about it.

REH

Rejoice and be glad, for your reward in heaven is great.

Matthew 5:12

LONG RANGE:

Play and/or sing a song, rejoicing.

5:00 AM	10:00 AM	2:00 PM	4:00 PM	5:00 PM
37	37	45	45	45

Cold all day!

One more month in this year. Life is like a vapor, per the Bible. So true.

However, it is a good vapor as long as you are with me.

I love you.

So proud of Dr's report yesterday for each of us.

PTL PTL.

Love to you.

REH

God has made everything appropriate in its time.

Jeremiah 3:11

LONG RANGE:

Name an event or circumstance in your life where God's timing was perfect.

5:00 AM	10:00 AM	2:00 PM	4:00 PM	5:00 PM
75	81	90	88	88

Praying for better health for you today.

Do hope you ARE BETTER.

It hurts me when you hurt.

I love you.

I will always (as long as able) take care of you – forever.

I love you.

REH

Do not be anxious about anything,

but in everything by prayer and pleading with thanksgiving

let your requests be made known to God.

Philippians 4:6

LONG RANGE:

Pray for your spouse's health today, physical health, but also mental, spiritual, emotional, and financial health as well.

5:00 AM	10:00 AM	2:00 PM	4:00 PM	5:00 PM
73	81	81	91	91

You are all I need.

You are my Sunshine.

I love you and just plain love being with you, here or elsewhere, it does not matter as long as I am with you.

REH

From the rising of the sun to its setting,

The name of the Lord is to be praised.

Psalm 113:3

LONG RANGE:

Grab some sunshine together today, even if only for a few moments.

5:00 AM	10:00 AM	2:00 PM	4:00 PM	5:00 PM
66	70	77	77	75

This is the day we have been looking for, you are free.

Hope we both get a good report from the doctor.

I love you.

I will always love you.

You are my BFF.

I love just being with you – I mean that.

I mean wherever.

REH

Jesus said,

"So if the Son sets you free, you really will be free."

John 8:36

LONG RANGE:

What does being set free mean to you?

5:00 AM	10:00 AM	2:00 PM	4:00 PM	5:00 PM
54	55	64	64	63

Cool all day.

Every day is THANKSGIVING for you and me.

We have so much to be thankful for.

Our God and each other, what more could you ask.

Love to you now and forever.

I love you.

PTL for you.

REH

I will give thanks to the Lord according to His righteousness

And will sing praise to the name of the Lord Most High.

Psalm 7:17

LONG RANGE:

Tell your spouse all the reasons you are thankful for him/her.

5:00 AM	10:00 AM	2:00 PM	4:00 PM	5:00 PM
63	66	72	73	72

Every day is Thanksgiving for US. God has blessed us beyond measure.

I just plain love you more and more as I stay with you more and more.

PTL PTL for you.

You are my life.

REH

"Enter His gates with thanksgiving,

And His courtyards with praise.

Give thanks to Him, bless His name."

Psalm 100:4

LONG RANGE:

Pray together, giving thanks to God for all He has done for you and for your spouse. Thank Him for your marriage and for the relationship you have with each other.

5:00 AM	10:00 AM	2:00 PM	4:00 PM	5:00 PM
48	61	73	73	70

Cool this morning.

Your self-imposed quarantine is really about over.

So glad for you.

You look so good. You are doing so much better.

PTL from us.

I love you more than ever.

REH

Jesus said,

"But as for you, when you pray, go into your inner room,

close your door, and pray to your Father who is in secret;

and your Father who sees what is done in secret will reward you."

Matthew 6:6

LONG RANGE:

Do you have a favorite place to pray in your home?

5:00 AM	10:00 AM	2:00 PM	4:00 PM	5:00 PM
57	66	75	75	72

A little cooler.

REH wants you to know, he loves you, so PTL that you are better each day.

Our God is so good to us. Let us PRAISE Him and serve Him and each other.

I love you.

REH

Make a joyful shout to the Lord, all you lands!

Serve the Lord with gladness;

Come before His presence with singing.

Psalm 100:1-2

LONG RANGE:

Sing a song of thanksgiving together.

5:00 AM	10:00 AM	2:00 PM	4:00 PM	5:00 PM
70	72	79	79	77

70's all the way.

Nothing in this note today but LOVE.

And there is plenty of it for you.

You make me Complete.

I love you and always will.

I love being with you.

REH

He made known to us the mystery of His will,

according to His good pleasure which He set forth in Him,

regarding His plan of the fullness of the times,

to bring all things together in Christ,

things in the heavens and things on the earth.

Ephesians 1:9-10

LONG RANGE:

What are some questions you might have for God when you get to Heaven?

5:00 AM	10:00 AM	2:00 PM	4:00 PM	5:00 PM
54	64	75	73	72

Home-time ending.

You are doing so good.

I am so proud of you.

I pray daily for your health.

God is awesome to us.

PTL PTL

I love you and just plain love being with you – wherever doing whatever.

REH

Beloved, I pray that in all respects you may prosper and be in good health, just as your soul prospers.

3 John 1:2

LONG RANGE:

Did your daily routine change during the pandemic? How has that changed your marriage?

5:00 AM	10:00 AM	2:00 PM	4:00 PM	5:00 PM
64	66	75	75	73

Cloudy.

Day 15 of quarantine.

Last day.

PTL PTL.

So thankful to God that you are better.

We both go to the doctor this week. We are doing great.

I love you.

Just plain love being with you.

REH

LOVE TO YOU.

Therefore I delight in weaknesses, in insults, in distresses,

in persecutions, in difficulties, in behalf of Christ;

for when I am weak, then I am strong.

2 Corinthians 12:10

LONG RANGE:

When was the last time you were weak? Did you experience God's strength during that time?

5:00 AM	10:00 AM	2:00 PM	4:00 PM	5:00 PM
63	70	75	75	73

Starting warm.

No more notes about quarantine because it is over.

PTL.

I am so happy for you and with you.

I love you and just plain love being with you – wherever.

I love you.

Dr. appointment in the morning, do not forget.

REH

Therefore you will joyously draw water

From the springs of salvation.

Isaiah 12:3

LONG RANGE:

Enjoy a glass of water together, thanking God for being the source of all water, and for providing Living Water for us eternally.

5:00 AM	10:00 AM	2:00 PM	4:00 PM	5:00 PM
68	72	75	73	73

Cloudy and may rain.

No more notes about Quarantine because it is over.

PTL.

Wonderful report yesterday for both of us.

We are blessed.

I love you and love just being where you are.

I miss you so at the office.

I LOVE YOU.

REH

Lord my God,

I cried to You for help, and You healed me.

Psalm 30:2

LONG RANGE:

Have you, or someone you know, ever been healed by God?

5:00 AM	10:00 AM	2:00 PM	4:00 PM	5:00 PM
46	46	45	43	43

Cold all day. Rain also.

Life is but a vapor (Bible).

So true.

Live it well.

Live so God is honored.

I love you and just love being with you.

I want you by my side always.

I love you.

REH

Now faith is the substance of things hoped for, the evidence of things not seen.

Hebrews 11:1 (NKJV)

LONG RANGE:

How has your faith grown during your marriage? How can it grow more?

5:00 AM	10:00 AM	2:00 PM	4:00 PM	5:00 PM
61	61	61	59	57

Rain all day.

Love that is just for you from me.

I love you.

You did well in your prayer.

You are a prayer warrior.

Ok? Ok!

REH loves EHH

REH

Be kindly affectionate to one another with brotherly love,
in honor giving preference to one another;
not lagging in diligence, fervent in spirit, serving the Lord;
rejoicing in hope, patient in tribulation, continuing steadfastly in prayer;
distributing to the needs of the saints, given to hospitality.
Romans 12:10-13 (NKJV)

LONG RANGE:

Do you have a group of friends who pray for you? Have you ever considered starting a prayer team?

5:00 AM	10:00 AM	2:00 PM	4:00 PM	5:00 PM
34	48	63	64	63

Cold all day.

Am glad yesterday is over. It was too long for you to be at office.

I just love you and I just love you being with me, wherever – home, office, church, store – wherever.

Just you and me.

I love you.

So glad you are feeling better and getting your strength back.

PTL.

God is so good to us.

REH

Yet those who wait for the Lord

Will gain new strength;

They will mount up with wings like eagles,

They will run and not get tired,

They will walk and not become weary.

Isaiah 40:31

LONG RANGE:

Are you tired or weary? Pray for each other.

5:00 AM	10:00 AM	2:00 PM	4:00 PM	5:00 PM
58	68	70	72	70

Warm all day. Rain in morning.

The house is coming along. It looks great.

I love it.

Also I love you and you being in this home.

Love to you.

REH

Wives, submit to your own husbands, as to the Lord.

Ephesians 5:22 (NKJV)

LONG RANGE:

How does submission play a role in your marriage? Read and discuss these verses too, Ephesians 5:25-28, because they speak to husbands.

5:00 AM	10:00 AM	2:00 PM	4:00 PM	5:00 PM
30	45	61	61	59

Still cool.

A few days till Christmas!

All I want for Christmas is YOU!

I love you and am so happy for you and me.

God is our refuge.

PTL for our life together.

We R ONE.

REH

God is our refuge and strength,

A very ready help in trouble.

Psalm 46:1

LONG RANGE:

How are you responsible for your spouse?

5:00 AM	10:00 AM	2:00 PM	4:00 PM	5:00 PM
39	48	61	61	57

Cold all day.

Another week has passed.

Today, the Lord's Day.

Let's worship God and be thankful.

I am thankful that God has put you in my life.

I love you more as I stay with you more.

PTL PTL for being so good to us.

I will give thanks to You, for You have answered me,

And You have become my salvation.

Psalm 118:21

LONG RANGE:

Pray together and thank God for your spouse and for your marriage and all it means to you.

5:00 AM	10:00 AM	2:00 PM	4:00 PM	5:00 PM
39	46	52	52	50

Cold all day.

Only a few more days after today and it will be Christmas!

So good just being with you – wherever.

I love you and want you with me all the time.

Love to Essie, my BFF.

REH

"An excellent wife, who can find her?

For her worth is far above jewels."

Proverbs 31:10

LONG RANGE:

Start a new Christmas tradition this year. And embrace the traditions you already have in place.

5:00 AM	10:00 AM	2:00 PM	4:00 PM	5:00 PM
48	59	72	72	70

Nice today.

LOVE, LOVE, LOVE.

Only love for you today.

That is the most important matter.

I thank God for you.

PTL we are ONE.

PTL we are under His watch.

PTL for everything.

REH

The Lord will guard your going out and your coming in

From this time and forever.

Psalm 121:8

LONG RANGE:

What does unconditional love mean to you?

5:00 AM	10:00 AM	2:00 PM	4:00 PM	5:00 PM
50	57	63	57	55

Cloudy. Some sunshine.

House is coming along.

It is looking so good.

I am proud of you and glad for you.

You deserve so much more.

I love you.

You are my BFF.

REH

For the gifts and the calling of God are irrevocable.

Romans 11:29 (NKJV)

LONG RANGE:

Do you feel called by God?

5:00 AM	10:00 AM	2:00 PM	4:00 PM	5:00 PM
55	61	73	72	70

Nice day today; fog this morning.

Nice trip yesterday. The cross was outstanding.

I just plain love you and love being with you.

If God is on our side, who can be against us.

REH

Your partner-in-life

"For I am convinced that neither
death, nor life, nor angels, nor principalities, nor things present,
nor things to come, nor powers, nor height, nor depth,
nor any other created thing will be able to separate us
from the love of God that is in Christ Jesus our Lord."
Romans 8:38-39

LONG RANGE:

Also read Ephesians 6:10-20. How does spiritual warfare impact your marriage?

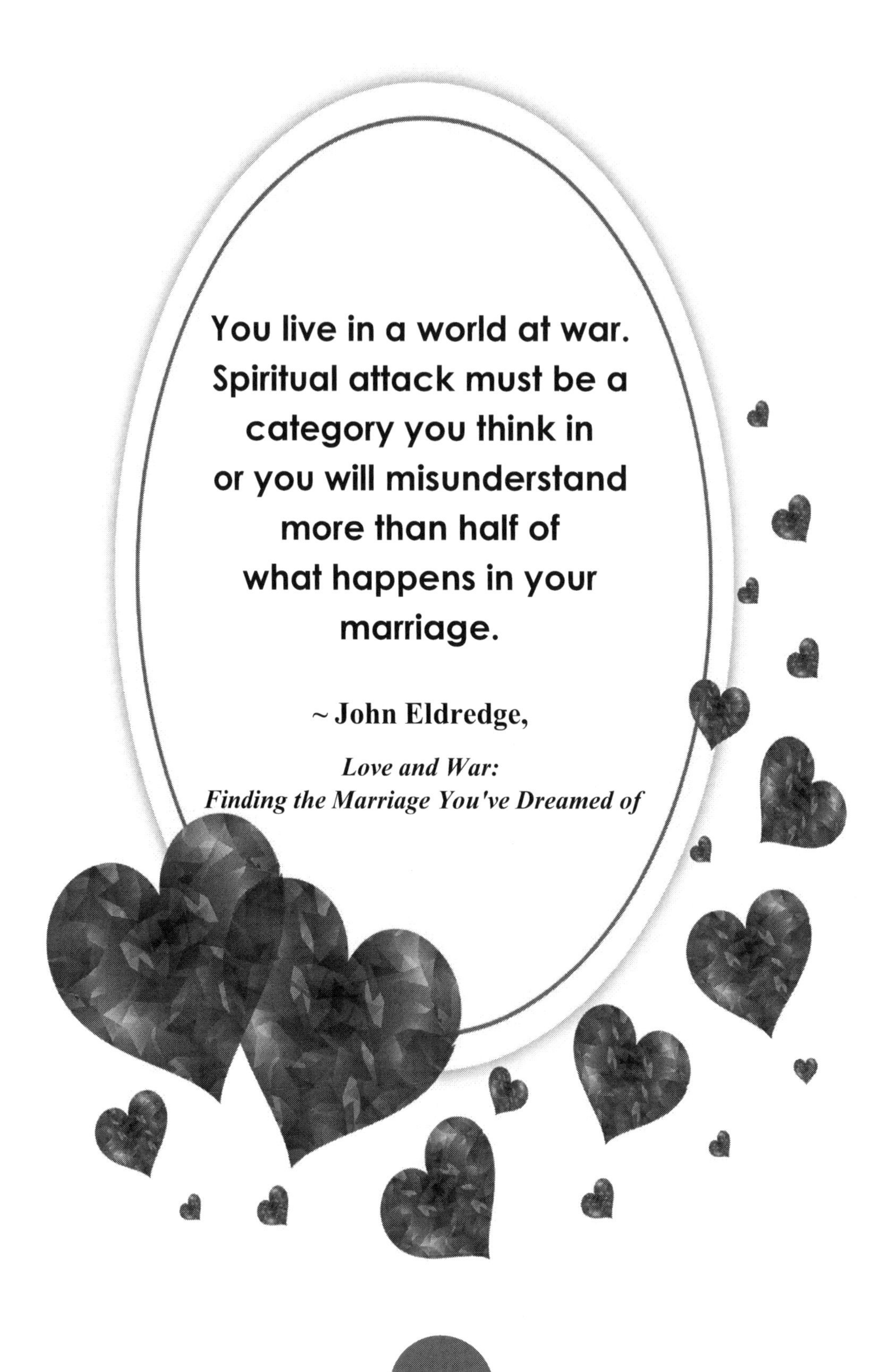
You live in a world at war.
Spiritual attack must be a
category you think in
or you will misunderstand
more than half of
what happens in your
marriage.
~ John Eldredge,
Love and War:
Finding the Marriage You've Dreamed of

For Unto Us
Is Born This Day
Jesus Christ
The Son Of
God

5:00 AM	10:00 AM	2:00 PM	4:00 PM	5:00 PM
23	32	46	48	46

Another COLD day.

This Christmas was great even the way we held it with the family.

You are so SPECIAL and have so many good ideas.

I love you.

I love being with you.

REH

For there is born to you this day in the city of David a Savior,

who is Christ the Lord.

And this will be the sign to you:

You will find a Babe wrapped in swaddling cloths, lying in a manger."

And suddenly there was with the angel a multitude of the heavenly host praising God and saying:

"Glory to God in the highest,

And on earth peace, goodwill toward men!"

Luke 2:11-14 (NKJV)

LONG RANGE:

Pray together and thank God for the gift of Jesus, and for the gift of your spouse, and for the gift of your marriage.

5:00 AM	10:00 AM	2:00 PM	4:00 PM	5:00 PM
28	39	54	55	52

Nothing here but love for you.

I love you.

I love being with you.

REH

Walk in love, just as Christ also loved you and gave Himself up for us,
an offering and a sacrifice to God as a fragrant aroma.
Ephesians 5:2

LONG RANGE:

What does it mean to you to live sacrificially in marriage?

5:00 AM	10:00 AM	2:00 PM	4:00 PM	5:00 PM
30	45	57	57	55

ATL 11 am – 3 pm: 48-55

Have a good and safe trip. I already miss you and you aren't even gone.

I love you and just plain love being with you.

House looks so good.

PTL PTL for us.

Our God is so good.

"Because he has loved Me, I will save him;

I will set him securely on high, because he has known My name.

He will call upon Me, and I will answer him;

I will be with him in trouble;

I will rescue him and honor him.

I will satisfy him with a long life,

And show him My salvation."

Psalm 91: 14-16

LONG RANGE:

Has God ever rescued you?

5:00 AM	10:00 AM	2:00 PM	4:00 PM	5:00 PM
45	54	64	63	63

Warmer than yesterday.

One more patch and I am through.

Love is going your way, from me and a lot of people.

You are SPECIAL.

You are a COMFORTER.

You are LOVED.

I love you.

I love being with you.

REH

Shout for joy, you heavens! And rejoice, you earth!

Break forth into joyful shouting, mountains!

For the Lord has comforted His people

And will have compassion on His afflicted.

Isaiah 49:13

LONG RANGE:

Pray together for anyone you know who might need God's comfort right now. If He leads you, offer comfort to them in person.

5:00 AM	10:00 AM	2:00 PM	4:00 PM	5:00 PM
61	48	48	48	46

Cold all day.

New week but old love for you. Old love that grows each day with you.

Old love that will never die.

I love you!

PTL PTL for our lives and our God.

PTL!

REH

The Lord appeared to him long ago, saying,

"I have loved you with an everlasting love;

Therefore I have drawn you out with kindness."

Jeremiah 31:3

LONG RANGE:

Show some random acts of kindness together to strangers this week.

5:00 AM	10:00 AM	2:00 PM	4:00 PM	5:00 PM
57	46	57	57	57

Cold all day.

Good morning to you.

You are my all.

You make me what I am.

You make me a better person.

PTL for you.

PTL for our God and His blessings.

I love you!

REH

Let me hear Your faithfulness in the morning,

For I trust in You;

Teach me the way in which I should walk;

For to You I lift up my soul.

Psalm 143:8

LONG RANGE:

What are your growth goals for next year?

5:00 AM	10:00 AM	2:00 PM	4:00 PM	5:00 PM
45	46	52	50	48

Cold all day.

Another week starting.

All is fine as long as I am starting and ending it with you.

You bring JOY into my life.

You are my life.

I love you SOOOOO much.

REH loves EHH now and forever.

PTL God is so good to you and me.

PTL.

REH

Now may the God of hope fill you with all joy and peace in believing,

so that you will abound in hope by the power of the Holy Spirit.

Romans 15:13

LONG RANGE:

How does your spouse bring JOY into your life?

Just another note of

LOVE

For you

From me.

REH

5:00 AM	10:00 AM	2:00 PM	4:00 PM	5:00 PM
30	39	50	52	48

Cold all day.

Great news from the doctor's office.

God is blessing you and I so much PTL PTL.

I thank God each day for you and putting you in my life.

We are ONE and we will serve God as ONE.

I love you.

I love being with you.

REH

May He grant you your heart's desire

And fulfill your whole plan!

Psalm 20:4

LONG RANGE:

Has God ever given you a heart's desire without you realizing you had that desire ahead of time?

5:00 AM	10:00 AM	2:00 PM	4:00 PM	5:00 PM
46	61	73	73	70

Nice today.

The celebrations are over.

However, life is a CELEBRATION with you!

I LOVE YOU!

So glad you are much, much better.

PTL – negative tests.

PTL for our life together.

Just plain PTL.

REH

Everything that has breath shall praise the Lord.

Praise the Lord!

Psalm 150:6

LONG RANGE:

How do you combat the holiday blues after all the celebrations are over?

5:00 AM	10:00 AM	2:00 PM	4:00 PM	5:00 PM
57	61	70	72	72

Let's go! Another week to start.

All is well as long as you and I are together, wherever, doing whatever.

Because I love you.

REH

The steadfast love of the Lord never ceases;

his mercies never come to an end;

they are new every morning;

great is your faithfulness.

Lamentations 3:22-23 (ESV)

LONG RANGE:

What are some sacrifices you've had to make in life? What was the outcome of the sacrifice?

5:00 AM	10:00 AM	2:00 PM	4:00 PM	5:00 PM
59	61	70	70	66

Rain early, then cloudy.

Love is just overflowing for you this morning. I cannot stop it.

I do not want to stop it. It is just what you do for me and with me that makes love stir up – unstoppable.

I love you.

PTL for our God and His care for you and me.

REH

Even to your old age, I am He,
And even to gray hairs I will carry you!
I have made, and I will bear;
Even I will carry, and will deliver you.
Isaiah 46:4 (NKJV)

LONG RANGE:

Does your love for each other feel unstoppable?

5:00 AM	10:00 AM	2:00 PM	4:00 PM	5:00 PM
50	50	57	61	61

2020 almost over.

New Year, New Life for us in a new office.

God is SO GOOD to us.

I just love having you by my side always.

I love you and always will.

REH

For you were called to freedom, brothers.

Only do not use your freedom as an opportunity for the flesh,

but through love serve one another.

Galatians 5:13 (ESV)

LONG RANGE:

Set goals for the New Year: life goals, couple goals, career goals, family goals. Put them on paper and refer back to them throughout the year.

* Note *

When we discuss hurts in this book, we are not talking about physical, emotional, or mental abuse. We condone none of that. If the hurts you are dealing with in your marriage are abuse, we urge you to get somewhere safe and seek help immediately. Reach out to someone safe.

If you don't feel you can trust anyone, here are some resources to get help:

If you are in immediate danger, call 9-1-1.

The National Domestic Abuse Hotline: **1-800-799-SAFE (7233)**

www.thehotline.org

Resource Recommendations

The Five Love Languages by Gary Chapman

Heaven by Randy Alcorn

All Things New by John Eldredge

Wild at Heart by John Eldredge

Love's Executioner by Irvin Yalom

12 Rules for Life by Jordan B. Peterson

The Living Legacy of Trauma by Janina Fisher

Maybe You Should Talk to Someone by Lori Gottlieb

Codependent No More by Melody Beatty (entire series of codependency books)

The Gift of Tears by Jeffrey Kottler

Change Your Brain, Change Your Life by Dr. Daniel Amen

Your Brain is Always Listening: Tame the Hidden Dragons That Control Your Happiness, Habits, and Hang-Ups by Dr. Daniel Amen

About the Author

Estelle “Essie” H. Herndon, is a Christ Follower, wife, mother, grandmother, great-grandmother and prayer warrior. She has worked alongside her husband, Robert, as his paralegal for over 50 years. They have been married 57 years.

Essie is active in her church. She teaches with her husband in Bible studies and leading small groups, helping with Women’s Ministries and Grief Ministries, from youth to young married adults.

She is also active in her community, having served on various boards over
the years.

Her family and friends are her hobbies. She and husband Robert enjoy traveling, which includes Georgia football games.

She truly tries to please God in her daily activities, always remembering where she has been in her past and how God has worked in her life for His Honor. She lives in Georgia.

Essie’s nonfiction book, ***Finding His Strength***, released in 2017, and her children’s books, ***KC’s Christmas Discovery***, and ***KC’s New Friend*** released in 2019 and 2020.

Loving life. Free in HIS strength!

Other Books by the Author

Available on Amazon, Kindle, and by request from most booksellers.

Thank you
for reading our books!

Look for other books
published by

www.TMPbooks.com

If you enjoyed this book
please remember to leave a review!

Made in the USA
Columbia, SC
08 May 2022